how to
Teach
for Exams

Sally Burgess
Katie Head

Longman

series editor:
Jeremy Harmer

Contents

Introduction

Who is this book for?

How to Teach for Exams is for all teachers of English who are currently teaching exam classes or expect to become involved in exam teaching in the future. The approaches discussed in this book should be of interest, both to teachers who are very experienced and to those who have been working for a relatively short time. Teacher trainers and trainees will also find useful and accessible ideas for skills teaching in *How to Teach for Exams*.

What is this book about?

It is difficult to imagine a career in foreign or second language teaching that does not, at some point, involve working with students who are preparing for an exam. Although an exam class may have a lot in common with other classes, the fact that students are preparing for an exam makes special demands on the teacher. *How to Teach for Exams* suggests how we might go about satisfying these demands.

The first two chapters establish the context of exam teaching and raise many of the most important issues. **Chapter 1** highlights some of the main differences between teaching an exam class and teaching a general language class, and considers what sort of teacher is best suited to exam teaching. It also looks at the first lesson of an exam course, and suggests ways of balancing teaching and testing as the course progresses. **Chapter 2** looks at exam course planning and choosing materials.

Chapters 3 to **7** deal with the skills and competencies tested in exams at intermediate level and above. Reading, writing, grammar and vocabulary, listening, and speaking are each focused on separately. These chapters offer a more detailed account of how each of these areas is typically tested in exams and suggest some teaching approaches. In each of these chapters there are activities (signalled by this icon 🙎) or sample lessons that can be adapted or used as points of departure to develop the teacher's own ideas. Finally, **Chapter 8** deals with the growing body of low-level exams aimed at less proficient learners.

The **Task File** at the back of the book is divided into sections corresponding to each of the chapters. This can be used in a number of ways. Teachers might like to look at the tasks before reading the chapter, while reading, or indeed after reading. The tasks can be done individually or used as a basis for discussion with colleagues or fellow trainees.

The **Exams overview** appendix summarizes the range of English language exams available internationally, explains how the Common European Framework (CEF) and the ALTE system provide a basis for comparing the levels of different exams, and includes information to help teachers find out more about these exams. Inside the back cover is a table comparing the main exams offered by the different boards, and their levels. The overview and table act as useful reference documents explaining the context of the exams discussed in the book.

How to be a successful exams teacher

- What is special about teaching an exam class?
- What qualities make a successful exams teacher?
- The first lesson of the course
- How to pace the course
- How to build students' exam skills
- How to balance teaching and testing in an exam class
- When to test

What is special
about teaching
a exam class?

Preparing students for an examination is a special responsibility. This is because exam results can have a significant effect on people's lives and careers; exams provide access to higher levels of education and open doors to certain professions. An offer of a place at a British or American university, for instance, may be conditional on achieving a specified IELTS or TOEFL grade; a pass in the Cambridge Certificate of Proficiency in English (CPE) is the passport to an English teaching job in some European countries. Even if a student is taking an exam for purely personal interest, or because their school requires them to, it is still an important event in their life and an opportunity to demonstrate success.

Yet, in many ways, teaching an exam class is not so different from teaching a general language class. The classroom activities and teaching techniques that work in general teaching will help to make a successful exams teacher. It is as important to build variety and fun into an exam course as it is to drive the students towards the goal of passing their exam. As in any course of study, it is also important to nurture the individual abilities of learners and attend to their needs and concerns. As shown in the examples in this book, the sorts of tasks that are set in formal examinations are often quite similar to the language practice tasks found in any good coursebook; indeed, in recent years, exam boards have made great efforts to develop assessment tasks and methods which reflect real-life uses of language.

Many teachers find that teaching an exam class is immensely satisfying. There are many reasons for this. The learners have a shared goal and strong motivation to succeed in their studies. The syllabus is clearly defined and there are lots of published materials (including, nowadays, some excellent

1

websites) available to supplement the main coursebook. On an exam course, it is easier to persuade students of the importance of homework, and of practising the skills in which they are weakest. And, at the end of all the effort, when the exam results are good, the teacher is rewarded by feeling that their teaching has contributed to the success enjoyed by the student.

On the other hand, exam teachers also need to be prepared for a range of possible frustrations and challenges. They may have less control and flexibility in determining the course content than with other types of course, and a great deal more marking of student assignments or practice tests. Teachers need to keep themselves informed on exam regulations and administrative details. It tends to be the teacher the students will ask when they want to know, for example, where the exam will take place, how long the listening test is, or whether dictionaries are allowed in the exam room. Teachers also usually have to cope with student anxiety in the weeks leading up to the exam; this may include counselling students who are not going to do well, perhaps because they enrolled unwisely or have not used their study time effectively.

What teachers need to know

Once teachers know they will be teaching an exam class, their first responsibility is to find out as much as possible about the format and content of the exam. The kinds of things they need to check are:

- How long is the exam?
- What skills are tested in the exam?
- What sorts of questions or tasks are used to test each skill?
- How many different parts are there to the exam?
- How much time is allowed for each part?
- What are the assessment criteria for each question or task type?
- How is the exam marked?
- How are the results presented?

This sort of information is not hard to find in exam coursebooks, handbooks, or on the website of the relevant exam board (see the Exams overview appendix on page 151). Every exam board now has its own presence on the web, where it is often possible to find not just general information about an exam, but also downloadable versions of the exam handbooks, syllabuses, and sample test questions. These websites are probably the most reliable and up-to-date source of information on particular exams.

In order to become familiar with the format of an exam, it is a good idea to work through at least one complete sample paper. Almost all exam coursebooks contain at least one practice test, designed to familiarize learners with the different sections of the exam, the types of questions asked, and the time allowed to complete each section or question. In addition to this practice test, there is usually some general information about the format of the exam elsewhere in the book, often near the beginning. By comparing the practice test to this more general information, the teacher should feel comfortable with the format of the exam.

Teachers need to know the date(s) when the exam will take place, and (eventually) the time, location, and procedural regulations. They may even find that they are personally responsible for the administrative procedures and paperwork connected with enrolling students for the exam; it goes without saying that these procedures need to be meticulously followed and are often time-consuming. Public examinations tend to be heavy on rules and regulations, in order to ensure that, no matter where in the world the exam is being taken, procedures are standardized and security is maintained. Even if there is a member of the institution's administrative staff who will deal with this, it is as well to make sure that the teacher liaises regularly with them and knows what they are doing, to ensure that candidate registrations are correctly processed and that information about exam dates, times, and locations reaches the right students at the right time.

As well as finding out about the exam itself, teachers also need to find out as much as they can about the students in the class and their reasons for taking the exam. This will influence course planning (see Chapter 2) and allow appropriate support to be provided for the students.

What qualities make a successful exams teacher?

The successful exams teacher is likely to be someone who:

- thinks that exams are useful and important.
- enjoys the discipline of teaching towards an exam, and manages their own and their students' time effectively.
- knows and understands the exam that they are teaching (including the necessary administrative details).
- listens to students' concerns and anxieties.
- gives honest and direct feedback on student performance.
- motivates students and fosters autonomous learning.

A positive attitude to exams

The following activity may be used, by experienced teachers as well as novices, to prompt reflection on their underlying attitude to exams.

> Call to mind some of the exams you have taken in your life, and make a list of reasons why exams are useful and important.
> Think about ways in which exams have had a positive influence on you as a learner.
> What do you like about taking exams?

To be a successful exams teacher, it is important to believe that exam preparation is a worthwhile exercise. Possible reasons for this might be:

> because they provide a target to aim at
> because they make me study harder
> because they make me revise and review what I have learned
> because they show other people what I am capable of
> because I can find out how good I am in comparison to other people
> because they give me qualifications which I can put on my CV
> because I like the feeling of knowing that I have achieved something

This activity, or something similar, can also be used at the start of a course to encourage students to think about why exams are useful and important. They can be asked to come up with a list of reasons, based on their own previous experience. Students can pool their ideas and write them on a poster for the classroom wall.

Enjoying the discipline of exam teaching

When preparing to teach for exams, we need to consider how willing we are to let the course content control us, rather than vice versa. Preparing students for an exam requires disciplined teaching and good time-management skills. Our task is to get all our students to the required level, usually within a limited period of time, and this tends to mean that there is less opportunity to be creative and spontaneous in making decisions about what we will teach. The course needs to be carefully planned in advance to ensure that there is adequate coverage of all the various exam tasks and sufficient practice of exam techniques, as well as time to review and consolidate knowledge of grammar and vocabulary and to build reading, writing, listening, and speaking skills. The factors to be taken into account when planning a course are considered in detail in Chapter 2. A well-organized person, who likes to spend time at the start of a course thinking about how to fit its various elements into the time available, is probably well suited to teaching for exams. Someone who likes to work on a lesson-by-lesson basis and enjoys the spontaneity of reacting to whatever comes up in class may not adapt so easily to the constraints of exam teaching.

Knowledge of the exam

As discussed on page 2, it is essential that we have a sound knowledge of the exam itself. Students will expect us to be able to answer accurately a wide range of questions about the exam. As we gain experience with a particular exam, we will be able to answer more such questions immediately. If we are teaching an exam for the first time, we should at least know where to go to find the answers. Then we can make a note of any question we are asked and tell the student that we will answer it in the next lesson (it is important to avoid giving out incorrect information about how the exam is presented and assessed). Teachers cannot afford to skimp on knowledge of the exam; students need to feel confident that they are in the hands of an authoritative source of information – on administrative, as well as academic matters. As the main point of contact with students, it may well be the teacher's job to tell them about enrolment procedures, arrangements for the day of the exam, regulations on what they can take with them into the exam room etc.

Keeping in touch with students

A different kind of teacher authority is involved in creating the sort of classroom atmosphere in which students can feel confident and happy about their learning. When there is a target to be reached in a limited time, and an expectation that a lot of hard work is involved, an effective teacher will remain aware of each student as an individual and monitor both the learning process, in terms of the student's motivation and effort, and their progress towards the desired outcome or exam result. Monitoring the process involves keeping in touch with our learners as people, and seeing that anxieties or difficulties are attended to. Most students start with a strong belief that they can succeed, and we need to support them by understanding and supporting that belief, especially when they are becoming anxious. We need to give students time to talk to us individually, let them tell us how they feel they are getting on, and tell them if we have any particular concerns about them. If a student appears to be doing badly or making little effort, the opportunity for an individual tutorial may uncover an explanation we had not thought of. Monitoring progress towards outcomes involves giving learners honest and direct feedback about how their performance measures up to the exam criteria. For example, if they are making language mistakes which will be harshly penalized in the exam, writing in an inappropriate style, or ignoring or misinterpreting task instructions, they need to be clearly warned of the consequences.

Maintaining motivation

Motivation tends to be high at the start of a course, but is difficult to sustain without some conscious effort to get the students to take personal responsibility for their own success. Good exam teachers know how to foster each learner's ability to recognize their own strengths and weaknesses, and are able to suggest strategies for building up those skills and knowledge areas which might otherwise let the student down in the exam. Helping learners to develop autonomous learning skills is important, since more independent learners will learn more and have a better understanding of their abilities than students who rely solely on what they are taught in class.

If entry to the exam class is barred to students whose starting level of English is not sufficiently high, the teacher's task is simpler and easier. We may, however, find ourselves teaching students whose ambition to succeed is matched neither by ability nor by motivation to do the necessary work. Parents and sponsors, as well as the students themselves, often have high expectations of the course, and may have paid a lot of money for it. While it is important for the teacher to support each student's belief in their ability to succeed, we must also be prepared to make it clear to the student – and perhaps to their sponsor or parents – how big the challenge is.

The first lesson of the course

Imagine a student arriving for the first lesson of an exam course. What would they be thinking about? Probably, they would be wondering who the other students are and what the teacher is like; they might want some information about the exam and how the course is going to prepare for it. They might be a bit worried about their current level of ability, the amount of work they will have to do, and whether they are going to be able to pass the exam. If it was their own choice to take this course, they may well also be quite excited, and eager to see the materials and find out what they are going to be doing.

There are some useful clues here to help teachers plan the content of the first lesson. It is worth spending some time on each of the following.

Getting to know the students

The kind of activity we use to start off the first lesson will depend on how well we already know the students, and how well they know each other. If we are all meeting for the first time, we will need to spend time learning names and helping students to feel at ease. We might do this by setting up an activity which requires them to talk to each other and find out information which they can then feed back to the whole group. Activities well-suited to such a purpose include interviewing a partner and then introducing their partner to the whole class, or talking to five classmates in order to find three things they have in common with each one, or a 'Find someone who …' activity (a version of this is described in Chapter 7, page 113).

If we already know the students and are known to them, this phase of the lesson can be quite short, although it may be useful to find out why they are attending this particular class and what they know about the exam. We may find out at this stage, for example, that we have some students who are not interested in the exam itself, but only in attending the class (some students think that they will learn more in an exam class than in a general class); or that we have students wanting to 'try' an exam which is much too difficult for them, and who will say that they just want to see what it is like. We may even have students who have been placed in the class but have no interest in or reason for doing an exam preparation course at all. For others, however, a university place, a job, or a financial sponsorship arrangement may depend on their exam result, or parents may be putting pressure on the student to succeed. It is as well to find out, as early as possible, what each student's level of motivation is, so that we can consider how we are going to deal with these various cases. It is also interesting to discover whether the students have taken an English exam before (and with what results) – indeed, whether any students have taken this exam before and failed it (if so, why) – and how the students feel about exams in general. These issues, and ways of responding to them, are further addressed in Chapter 2.

Introducing students to the exam

An introduction to the format and content of the exam is likely to form a major part of the first lesson. Most students know very little beyond the name (and usually the level) of an exam, and it is helpful to give them a clear picture of what they are aiming for. The main information can be prepared on handouts which can be taken away and referred to throughout the course. For the lesson itself, the same information is best presented to the whole class, either on the board or using overhead projection.

Students need immediate information on the date(s) when the exam will be held, when and how to enrol and pay the exam fee, the format of the exam (the number and type of different papers), and some sample questions showing which skills are tested and how.

An overview of the different components of a particular exam can often be found at the front of coursebooks, as well as on the website or exam handbook of the relevant exam board. It is often presented as a grid showing the name of each paper, its length, and a brief list of the different task types. Although it can be difficult to absorb at such an early stage of the course, this is important reference information for students.

To accompany an exam overview presentation, some sample questions can be practised, to illustrate the different task types on each paper. Alternatively, pages from the handbook can be copied and a set of quiz questions prepared, so that students have to scan the handbook pages for essential information such as: *How long is the speaking exam? How many different question types are there in the reading section?* The aim is to give a flavour of the exam, not to present complete papers, so it is necessary to be selective. A sample writing task can be set as a first homework.

Introducing the course and establishing ground rules

Different aspects of course organization, such as how the course is paced, how learning will be monitored, and when practice tests will be used, will have been considered in the pre-course planning. It is sensible to explain these aspects to students in the first lesson, so that they can appreciate the way that the course is organized and how it will prepare them for the exam.

It can also be a wise move to make clear in the first lesson what the teacher's own expectations are. Ground rules such as how much homework the students are expected to do, whether they should bring dictionaries to class, and how they should make up the work if they miss a lesson, should be clearly established. It can be a good idea to make a learning contract with the class, and put it up on the wall where it can be easily referred to. This is a statement of both the teacher's and the learners' expectations of each other. Students preparing to take an exam need to understand that they will have to work on their own as well as in class, and that the hardest work may need to be done on areas of language that are least appealing, such as grammar and writing.

How to pace the course
The build-up to an exam may be long or short, depending on the type of exam and on the time available. A course of two hours per week over ten weeks, for example, will be able to do little more than familiarize students with the exam format and give advice on techniques for answering the questions, while a course of 120 hours or longer will allow a more gradual build-up to the exam, with time for teaching as well as testing. Most exam coursebooks are designed for courses of around 120 to 150 hours.

However long or short the course, careful planning is essential to ensure that the students are ready at the right time to perform at their best, and to take account of the highs and lows which are a natural part of the journey towards the day when they sit the exam. Typically, progress does not happen in a straight line but in a series of waves. Upward swells of enthusiasm will inevitably give way to downward drifts when confidence falters, boredom sets in, or energy evaporates. This is something to be aware of and allow for in pacing, since it is likely to affect the teacher as well as the students.

Once the teacher knows how much class time is available, it is a good idea to prepare an outline plan for the course on a one-page grid, showing the number of weeks and the skills, topics, tasks, exam components etc. which will be the focus of each week's work. This allows a complete overview and makes it easier to ensure that the course structure includes everything that has to be covered. In planning, teachers will want to check that the time allowed for practising the different language skills is fairly balanced, and that there is some scope for recycling and reviewing previously learned skills and knowledge as the course progresses.

How to build students' exam skills

Exams tend to be associated in learners' minds with a great deal of pressure and anxiety, so it is important for us to help them maintain a sense of control and to foster skills which make them better able to cope. Our own memories of what it was like to be preparing for an exam will be an invaluable aid to thinking about the kind of support we can provide for our students. A helpful exercise for teachers planning to run an exam course can be to recall and note down any good study habits that they developed in the context of their own experience of taking exams.

Developing good study habits

Most learners recognize that they cannot depend totally on their teacher to get them through an exam, and that they must do a lot of work for themselves. However, they do not always know how to do this, and often lack the organizational skills and discipline required. We can help them by encouraging the development of good study habits, both in and out of the classroom. Here are the sorts of things that students should be doing:

- **spending some regular out-of-class time working on their English** – Steady commitment is a much surer guarantee of success than occasional bursts of activity.
- **reviewing what they did in class and making a note to ask about anything that was not clear** – Failure to do this means that they don't know what they don't know, and neither does the teacher.
- **learning to use reference books such as dictionaries and grammars intelligently** – Some teachers like to ban reference materials (especially dictionaries) from the classroom, to discourage students from over-dependence on them. However, there is much value in the opposite approach: encouraging the use of dictionaries and grammar reference books, and building some study-skills training into the early part of the course to teach students how to use them properly.
- **finding a time and place to study where they can concentrate and not be distracted** – Students' home circumstances may make it difficult for them to study properly. It is a good idea to discuss this with each of the students and advise them appropriately. They will be reassured by knowing that we are aware of any difficulties that they are having with finding time and space to study. There is so much activity around people

nowadays, and so much environmental noise, that their powers of concentration and tolerance of silence are often quite low. Some students may not have experienced before the feeling of sitting in a silent exam room, working on a question paper for an hour or longer and not being able to get up, make noise, and move around. Becoming comfortable with this constrained situation can be an important part of exam preparation.

* **organizing their paperwork so that they can review their work easily and get a sense of their own progress** – Too often, completed work just gets pushed into a file or folder, never to be looked at again. It is worth spending time with students, helping them to set up retrieval systems, so that both they and we can review and monitor their learning over time. Some assignments may also function as useful revision material, as the exam draws near.

* **monitoring their own use of language, identifying and correcting their own mistakes** – This relates both to the previous point and to the one made earlier about learning to use reference materials. There are a number of suggestions for helping learners to monitor and correct themselves throughout this book.

* **keeping an independent learning record or diary** – If we want to monitor this, we can produce a simple form for each student, on which they record any work done in their own time, and which they periodically discuss with us. Another option is to ask them to keep a learning diary. This may appeal to some students, but can be time-consuming both for them to write and for us to read.

* **asking for help with anything that is worrying them** – Noting down questions and problems which learners can't resolve on their own, and then asking someone for help, is a good study habit. However, it is important to know where to go for help and advice, and to make sure that the right sort of people are available to talk to learners.

* **practising and using the language as much as possible** – Some students think that they can learn all they need to know for an exam by studying books and doing practice exercises and tests. This may have been true in the past but is much less true today, with most current exams designed to test the kind of language used in real communicative contexts.

Coping with the build-up of pressure

Pressure affects people in different ways. Research shows that, up to a point, stress acts as a positive motivator and is even necessary to get things done (as the authors have found in writing this book!), but that once it goes beyond that point it tends to have a negative and harmful effect on a person's ability to cope. This effect will be different for each individual.

It is important to be alert to signs that a learner is having difficulty coping with the pressure of exam preparation. For example, the student might be failing to hand in work, or doing work which is suddenly of a lower standard than before. They may miss lessons, or fail to pay attention when they are present; or they may be seen studying in the library at all hours. Some students show stress in unsurprising ways, such as looking pale or tired, while others express it by behaving aggressively or insolently, lying or cheating, or becoming isolated from the group.

Of course, there could be many other reasons why a student is showing symptoms such as these, which is why it is important to talk to them privately to try and discover what is going on. The best approach for us as teachers is to start by telling the student that we have noticed a particular behaviour and that this is concerning us. If we act supportively and offer the time to listen, the student should feel able to talk. Even if nothing of significance emerges at the time, they may come back later if there is really a problem, and ask us to help or advise.

Some teachers feel that they should never show any anxiety or concern to their learners, in case this leads to a breakdown of confidence. However, there is a lot to be said in favour of an alternative perspective; many teachers feel it is important to be as open to our learners as we expect them to be to us, within the constraints of professional propriety and respect. If we are unsure how to proceed in relation to our concerns about a particular student, it can be helpful to take advice from a trusted colleague (while bearing in mind possible confidentiality issues).

At a more general level, it is a good idea to build into the course some opportunities to raise issues relating to the maintenance of a healthy life–work balance, and how to cope when the pressure starts to build up. There are various ways of doing this, for example, by finding a relevant reading text and discussing it, through role-plays of situations in which students are having difficulty coping with pressure (such as not sleeping, getting frequent headaches, feeling that they can't remember things) and are discussing their problems with advisors, or through an open discussion of strategies for coping with the stress of exam preparation.

One of the things that students worry most about is what is actually going to happen on the day of the exam. Just as one of the ways in which exam teaching is special is that the teacher needs to be very knowledgeable about the exam they are teaching, so this is correspondingly true for the students; the more they know what to expect, the less anxious they will be about turning up on the day.

How to help learners do their best on the day

This exercise – useful for teachers – can be done with students, in the last few days before the exam. It is a great confidence-builder.

> Imagine that a close friend or relative of yours is taking an exam tomorrow. What advice would you give them?
>
> Note down your 'golden rules' for ensuring that they give themselves the best chance of doing well.

Divided into groups, each group of students is asked to come up with ten golden rules for passing the exam. The class can then negotiate and pick the ten best from all the ideas collected.

Here are **ten golden rules for written exams** …
- Arrive in good time for the exam.
- Bring a spare pen and pencil.
- Look through the whole exam paper before you start to answer the questions.
- Read and follow the instructions carefully.
- Divide your time sensibly between all the questions.
- If there is a choice of possible answers, consider all the choices before making your decision.
- If you are writing an essay, keep to the point and show the examiner what you know.
- Don't take risks. If you are not sure of a particular word or grammar point, try saying it in a different way.
- Leave time at the end to check your work.
- Write legibly and tidily.

… and **ten golden rules for speaking exams**
- Arrive in good time.
- Find someone to talk to in English while you are waiting to go into the exam room.
- When the examiner greets you, reply appropriately (e.g. *Hello. My name is …*).
- When you sit down, take your time to make yourself comfortable. The examiner will not begin until you say you are ready.
- Listen carefully to what the examiner says, and ask him/her politely to repeat it if there is something you don't understand.
- Show the examiner what you can do. Don't just give one-word answers to questions.
- If you are taking the exam together with another candidate, be sure to give each other enough time to speak.
- Remember that the examiner wants you to do well. He/She is not trying to scare you or trip you up.
- At the end of the exam, thank the examiner, and say goodbye.

How to balance teaching and testing in an exam class

If the course has very limited class time, the teacher will be able to do little more than familiarize students with the exam format and teach them some exam techniques. Given more time, it is wise, for a number of reasons, to build some formal tests into the course plan.

Firstly, students enrolled on an exam course expect to do lots of practice tests. Indeed, some students expect the whole course to consist of doing one practice paper after another, and the fact that this does not happen can be a source of great frustration for such individuals.

A second and more pedagogically valid reason, is that testing prepares students for the experience of reading, writing, listening, or speaking under exam conditions, and of following exam procedures. It is as well to make class testing as similar to exam testing as possible, by sticking strictly to time limits, refusing to allow noise, insisting that answers are transferred to an official answer sheet (as is required by some exam boards), and so on.

Thirdly, these practice tests can be marked using the formal exam criteria. This enables both teacher and students to see how well the students are doing. However, we need to be careful here if we have a class of students who are rather weak, since too much focus on the pass level can highlight their inadequacies and have a negative impact on their state of mind.

The final section of this chapter considers *when* it is appropriate to test students. The main ongoing work of the course, however, should be focused on teaching, rather than testing. The kind of teaching that is required will depend very much on the abilities of the learners, and on the extent of the gap between their current level and the level of the exam. Finding an appropriate balance between teaching and testing in a given class will depend on whether it would be described as 'weak', 'average to good', or 'strong', in respect of the likelihood of its students reaching the level required to pass the exam that they are enrolled for.

The weak class

This class often has ambitions above its abilities. There are always some students who enrol for an exam despite the best advice of their teachers, or perhaps because there is pressure from a parent or institution. These students tend to lack essential knowledge and language skills, so the priority has to be teaching rather than testing. The aim is still to get them through the exam, but this is combined with a realistic assessment of their capabilities and a programme of teaching which recognizes their limitations and fills in the gaps in their basic knowledge of the language.

The average-to-good class

This is a class of students who have already covered all the basic language patterns and vocabulary and have reasonably well-developed skills, although writing is often weaker than their other skills, perhaps due to lack of pressure to practise. They still have plenty of work to do, but their need is to review and consolidate what they should already know. They also need to practise those skills, normally reading and writing, which tend to be more emphasized in exams than on non-exam courses. Regular testing should have the effect of proving to these students what they can achieve through steady hard work, and provide a positive challenge.

The strong class

Occasionally, we may meet a class of students who are ready to take the exam with little special preparation. They are already up to the required level, and there is not a lot to teach them beyond familiarization with the exam format and how to answer questions in the best way possible. This sort of class can sometimes be hard to motivate, since everything to do with the exam is quite easy for them. Regular testing will reassure them of this fact and stop them from worrying that they should be doing more to prepare for the exam. Teaching can concentrate on challenging them further in areas where they can demonstrate above-average ability, such as vocabulary range, stylistic sensitivity, and pronunciation and intonation. They can be shown how the marking criteria credit exceptional ability and how those who pass at the top level are distinguished from those who achieve an average pass.

When to test All students in exam classes need to be tested, at different stages of their course, for various purposes.

Pre-testing

Pre-testing takes place either before the course starts or in the first week of a term or semester. It is a way of determining what a student's abilities are before they begin to prepare for an exam. Pre-testing provides information which can be used to advise a student on which exam they should be taking (if this is not yet decided), and on their chances of achieving the required result. It also gives students an idea of what the exam is like, and how close they are to achieving the necessary level.

Sample questions from different parts of the exam may be used for pre-testing, and can be marked using the formal exam criteria. These will allow us to predict how well the student is likely to do even without preparation, which is useful information for the teacher.

Revision testing

The purpose of revision testing is to check that learners can apply their knowledge and skills to the sorts of tasks that will appear on the exam paper. Revision tests help to familiarize students with the various task types as well as indicating how well they are doing. They should reflect the work recently done in class and can be set at regular intervals throughout the course (such as after completing a unit) or at the end of each term.

Mock exams

The main reason for giving a mock exam is to reduce anxiety about procedural issues, such as how to complete a written exam in the time available, or what the examiner will ask you to do in the speaking exam. It provides an experience of exam-taking which can be reviewed afterwards with the students, and which allows them to identify and discuss things that might be worrying them about the exam day. Ideally, an authentic past paper should be used for a mock exam; some exam boards publish these or make them available for download from their website. It is important to replicate exam-room conditions and timings as far as possible; in order to authenticate the experience, the teacher will need to stop behaving like a class teacher and start behaving like an invigilator (during the exam) and an examiner (when marking). As 'invigilator', the teacher must follow the rules of conduct stated in the exam regulations, for example, checking that students' mobile phones are switched off, controlling start and finish times, and refusing to answer questions. As 'examiner', the teacher should mark strictly according to the formal criteria set by the exam board, and award grades.

Conclusions   In this chapter we have:
- looked at similarities and differences between exam courses and other courses.
- discussed some reasons why teaching exam classes can be satisfying.
- identified the qualities needed to be a successful exams teacher.
- considered some of the practical things an exam teacher needs to know.
- considered what to do in the first lesson of an exam course.
- explained why it is important to pace the course.
- pointed out that learners need to take responsibility for their own learning, and presented ideas for fostering good study habits.
- suggested some ways of helping students cope with exam pressure, both during the course and on the day of the exam.
- commented on different levels of exam groups and their different needs with respect to teaching and testing.
- considered the purpose of formal tests, and when they should be used on an exam course.

How to plan a course and choose materials

- Factors to take into account when planning
- How these factors affect course planning
- How to choose materials for a particular course

When preparing to plan a course, the exam itself must be a primary influence. It is important to get a good understanding of the language level and purpose of the exam. Many exams can be directly related to the **Common European Framework** (CEF) system of levels or to the **ALTE** system of levels, both of which are referred to in the course of this book. The Exams overview appendix, on page 151, gives a brief explanation of the CEF and ALTE level systems; it also lists the various exams and their website addresses, where it is possible to find additional and updated information on them.

Apart from the exam itself, key factors to consider relate to the students, the time available, and access to resources such as computers, the Internet, and audiovisual equipment. The following checklist may help when thinking about who the **students** are, and where and why they are preparing for the exam:

- How many students will there be in the class?
- How old are the students?
- Will the students be attending a school or a private class?
- Do they share the same language and cultural background?
- Are there any specific linguistic or cultural factors to take into account?
- Are all the students in the class preparing for the exam?
- Why are they preparing for the exam?
- Have they taken any public English exams before?

Once we have identified the students, we need to consider how much **time** is available, both inside and outside class, between the beginning of the course and the exam. The following questions may prove useful:

- How many months will the course last?
- Is this the last course students will take before sitting for the exam?
- How many hours a week will I be teaching these students?
- How much time will they have for independent study or homework?

Finally, the availability of **resources**, materials, and support – both for the teacher and for the students – needs checking, as follows:

- Will students have access to computers and relevant software at school and/or at home?
- Will they have access to the Internet at school and/or at home?
- Are there video facilities in the school, and how often will teacher and students be able to use them?
- Does the school supply any of the course materials (e.g. class sets of dictionaries, grammars, CD-ROMs, online courses)?
- How many course components can the students afford to buy themselves?

Having answered each of the questions above, we should be able to build up a profile of our class, as in the following example:

FCE Class 1   10 students in group
                                                    Aged 13 to 16
                                                 All Polish speakers

7 taking exam in June next year (on parents' instigation)
1 planning to take exam in December
2 not yet decided to take exam
8 have passed PET
Can do about 3 hours' homework a week
32 weeks or 180 hours+ class time available
No computer or Internet access at school but some home access
Video room in school can be used once a week
School supplies dictionaries
Students can buy coursebook and workbook

How these factors affect course planning

How we design a course will be influenced by factors associated with the students, the context of their study, and the availability of time and other resources. These will also affect selection of the materials to be used.

Class size

The number of students in a group obviously has a significant impact on methodology. At one extreme we might find very large classes (30 plus) in contexts such as universities or state-run schools and, at the other, private one-to-one exam classes.

In the large class context, most classroom management decisions need to be made in advance. In the one-to-one or small class context, on the other hand, the teacher can very effectively adopt a test–teach–test approach. For example, a writing task might be set for homework. In a subsequent class, when reading and commenting on the written work, it might emerge that most students are having difficulty with participle clauses. The teacher will immediately do some work on that area and then set more homework to check that effective learning has taken place.

Class size will also determine how many pieces of written work can be set and marked and how often speaking skills can be monitored on an individual basis. In large classes, it will almost certainly be necessary to set up student–student monitoring of speaking and written work, as well as allowing time outside class for marking and record keeping. In one-to-one and small group contexts, a lot of marking and commenting on students' writing and speaking can be done during the lessons themselves.

Age

A student's age may have an impact on motivation, and this will have implications for course design, classroom procedures, and materials. Enrolling in an exam class and registering for the exam itself is usually something adults decide to do themselves. As a result, they may be highly motivated and willing to put in the necessary effort. This means that the teacher can plan a course geared towards active and committed adult learners. In the case of younger learners, the decision to take the exam is often made for them by a parent. In some cases, the student may resent having to prepare for it or feel pressured by parental ambitions. If an exam class is made up of young learners like these, it is important to ensure that there are plenty of entertaining activities like songs and games to bolster motivation. Parents can be reassured by evidence that their son or daughter is completing the exercises in the coursebook and workbook. Regular progress testing may help to convince parents that the teacher is doing a good job, and may also help to motivate learners.

Students' ages may also affect the decision to adopt an approach with an emphasis on autonomous learning. A course with a lot of student-produced tasks or project work may go down better with younger learners who will, in some cases, have met this approach at school. Older people who are more accustomed to a traditional teacher-fronted classroom environment, may show resistance to an exam course in which they are expected to participate in decision-making and materials design. Even so, taking responsibility for one's own development is an essential element in exam preparation. It is worth persevering in this area with students, even if there is a certain amount of initial unease. There are suggestions throughout this book as to how students might be encouraged to take on such responsibilities.

In terms of materials, it may be the case that younger learners respond very positively to electronic media while older adults might find these less appealing, possibly because they associate computer use with the work environment and not with language learning. Some older adults may even lack sufficient computer literacy to make materials in electronic format a viable option. At the same time, it is the adult learner who is more likely to have a computer and the wherewithal to purchase software.

Context

Whether the students are studying in an English-speaking environment, or in an environment where their first language prevails, may also influence exam course planning.

Students who are studying in countries such as the UK, Ireland, the USA, Australia, Canada, or New Zealand will almost always be members of exam classes in which many language backgrounds and cultures are represented. This will make class discussion stimulating, but it will also mean that a focus on the particular problems of any one group will be inappropriate. For example, extensive remedial pronunciation work geared to the needs of Spanish speakers will probably bore and frustrate a class in which speakers of Asian and Scandinavian languages are also represented. Students preparing for an exam in their own countries, on the other hand, can often take advantage of the language-specific materials some publishers make available, as well as benefiting from the expertise of teachers who understand their first language and the particular difficulties with English that it may bring. In a setting where there is minimal exposure to English outside the classroom, the teacher will want to devote plenty of class time to listening and speaking, especially to pronunciation (see Chapters 6 and 7, as well as the companion volume in this series, *How to Teach Pronunciation*).

An English-speaking environment means ready access to native speakers of English, as well as to TV, radio, and cinema in English, and may therefore reduce the need for listening and speaking preparation and practice, and for the grading of that preparation and practice. It will also mean that students can play an active role in producing listening and reading materials for classroom use, though in the age of the Internet this is something that almost anyone can now do, regardless of where they happen to be living.

Linguistic and cultural factors

An obvious issue at the planning stage in the case of monolingual groups is the language and cultural background of the students. Awareness of particular problems experienced by speakers of the language concerned will probably prompt the teacher to programme additional work on these areas, perhaps making use of materials produced specifically for that context. Most of these materials are geared towards the grammar and writing components of the exam concerned. If the students' first language differs markedly from English in some respect (e.g. the article system, verb tenses, word order), then one would expect to find extra practice on these areas.

Cultural factors may have more subtle implications too. Students from some cultural backgrounds may expect the teacher to lead and control all classroom interaction and may be reluctant to work with other students. In such cases, it will be necessary to convince students that pair and group work plays an important role in exam preparation.

The demands of the exams themselves may be culturally alien to the students and may therefore need to be introduced carefully and handled with sensitivity. For example, some students may be unused to writing discursive essays in which they express an opinion. Similarly, paired-speaking tasks may pose a particular problem because expression of disagreement is unacceptable in the culture or, on the other hand, because a more confrontational approach to discussion is the norm. It is sensible to devote more time to conversational strategies, such as expressing opinions or expressing polite agreement and disagreement, in contexts like these.

Finally, most exams inevitably make certain assumptions about cultural background knowledge and we may find that our students are unfamiliar with some of the ideas and concepts that are taken for granted in skills work. In this case, a certain amount of cultural input can be included in the course plan, possibly drawing on the Internet as a source. Activities can be prepared in which students research topics such as family life, celebrations, housing, education, and so on as an adjunct to the information provided in texts they encounter in the coursebook. Some teacher's books accompanying exam courses suggest web sources of this type.

Time factors

Obviously, the time available has considerable impact on the choice of methodology and of materials. The amount of time students have to prepare for an exam can vary enormously. This is sometimes related to the kind of exam (see the Exams overview appendix) students are intending to take; some exams are designed to require minimal preparation beyond a general English language course, while others such as the Cambridge ESOL exams may have a build-up time of two or even three years.

Where only very limited time is available, the teacher will want to streamline preparation by making sure students become thoroughly familiar with the exam format. Most of the work performed in class and set to be done out of class will be exam-focused, and it may be advisable to assign an exam handbook or workbook (see below), as well as making use of practice test materials in conventional and/or electronic formats.

Where there are longer periods of exam preparation, the teacher is more likely to opt for a gradual build-up to the exam. Many publishers now offer two- or three-level courses geared to specific exams; the lower levels offer less emphasis on explicit exam preparation, while coursebooks and workbooks intended for use in the final year of exam preparation are largely dedicated to exam-style tasks and advice on strategies and procedures.

The amount of time that we expect to see our students will also affect course design. We may have one-to-one classes in which we see the student for only an hour a week. In contrast are intensive courses in which students attend class three to six hours a day, five days a week. In between is the situation in many private language schools, where students come to class for between three and five hours a week.

In the case of the one-to-one, one hour a week class, it is advisable to assign many tasks as homework, particularly in the case of reading and writing. The intensive course scenario, on the other hand, leaves students with little time (or energy!) for independent study; it is also a context in which the teacher needs to make sure that there are changes in pace and a good variety of topics and activities. Students are then more likely to remain interested and motivated.

Composition of the class

We may find ourselves teaching a class in which some of the students are preparing for an exam and others are not. In such circumstances, the teacher will need to give due attention to general skills and language development alongside exam-style tasks. Fortunately, many exam tasks reflect good classroom practice and can be used with general English students without their having to master complex and unfamiliar procedures. Depending on the proportion of exam and non-exam students in a class, the teacher can change the emphasis given to the various sections of each unit in the coursebook, possibly assigning all exam-specific work as homework or asking exam students to buy a workbook or handbook for self-access use.

The students' exam experience

Previous exam experience may mean that we do not need to give as much emphasis to exam techniques and procedures as we would with students preparing for their first English exam. If students are taking an exam for the first time, or after many years away from formal study, it may be necessary to devote quite a lot of class time to study skills and learner training, as well as to the specific techniques needed for the exam.

As a summary of what has been discussed so far, the following example scenario shows how decisions might be taken:

Student profile
- Three sixteen-year-old Spanish-speaking girls preparing for the Cambridge ESOL Certificate of Proficiency in English in Spain.
- Little variation in level (all three girls took Cambridge ESOL FCE two years ago. Grades A or B). All have been registered for the exam by their parents. All three are concurrently doing their final year of secondary school and preparing for university entrance. All are highly motivated.
- All three have their own computers.
- Began course in early October; will take the exam in early June. Approximately 32 classes (one class a week (3 hours) Saturday mornings). All are willing and able to devote approximately 6 additional hours a week to homework and study.

Planning Decisions
- Overall approach 'Test–Teach–Test'
- Class time divided between listening and speaking with grammar and vocabulary revision and extension
- Reading and writing work to be done outside class, also Use of English exercises (CD-ROM)
- Discussion, marking, and review of homework in class

How to choose materials for a particular course

An important part of course planning is the selection of appropriate materials. Since most teachers have busy schedules, in which they teach between twenty and thirty hours a week, at least part of what they do in exam classes may well involve using published materials. However, it is often worthwhile for teachers to find time to produce materials specifically for the needs of their own students.

Here is a summary of the types of materials that teachers can use:

Print materials
- coursebooks
- workbooks
- exam handbooks
- practice test books
- supplementary books (dictionaries and grammars)

Electronic materials
* materials on CD-ROM
* online materials
* video or DVD

'Home-made' materials
* the teacher's materials
* the students' materials

When choosing materials for a course, it is helpful to analyse the issues according to the topic areas discussed in the rest of this chapter.

Audience

* **Is the course intended for teenagers or adults?** The publishers usually indicate this on their web pages and in their catalogues, as well as on the covers of the materials themselves. If this not the case, the fact that students are expected to discuss, read, and write about weighty topics such as human rights or war would be a good indication that the course is intended for adults. Materials directed at young teenagers, on the other hand, take much of their topic content from popular culture. They often tend to have a lighter-hearted approach to language and skills practice, including games, cartoons, and even pop songs.
* **Is the course aimed at high-achievers or average learners?** Again, this is often indicated, especially if the course is intended for candidates who are going for a grade higher than a pass. Exam-level texts and tasks will occur early, and the later units might go beyond the demands of the exam itself to include language and skills work at a slightly higher level.
* **Is it geared to exam students only?** Publishers sometimes avoid mentioning the exam so as not to limit the potential market. If a coursebook is geared exclusively to learners who are preparing for the exam, descriptions of exam tasks, procedures, and strategies will be given prominence. There will also be fewer, if any, general non-exam activities and a great deal more specific exam preparation. Most language practice will involve exercises that are similar to the part of the exam that tests grammar and vocabulary. Skills development will also often be achieved through exam-style tasks. There may also be exam-style tests throughout the book and a practice exam at the end.
* **Is the course intended for use in the final lead-up to the exam itself?** If this is not the case, there will be more space devoted to general English, and language and tasks will be carefully graded starting well below the level of the exam itself. If, on the other hand, the course is intended for use in the last year of exam preparation, there will be a lot of very focused and specific exam practice at or slightly above the level of the exam. There will also be at least one practice exam.

Content and format

One of the first things to discover is how many components there are and what they contain. Apart from the units themselves, **coursebooks** usually include banks of exercises to check how successfully learners have absorbed

21

the content, normally interspersed with the units themselves. The publishers may also include (at the back or in the middle of the book) various kinds of additional material such as a grammar reference, a writing reference with model answers, banks of visuals for speaking practice, communicative activities, practice tests, phrasal verb lists, and so on.

Several publishers offer courses made up of **modular components** intended to prepare students for each exam paper (Reading, Writing, Use of English, Listening, Speaking) or each of the areas tested. The rationale for this approach is that a flexible course can be designed where due emphasis is given to those parts of the exam that we consider to be particularly taxing for our students. This modular approach also allows us to design a course in which we use material from different publishers in the same exam class, or use some published elements and write the rest of the materials ourselves.

All coursebooks are accompanied by a **teacher's book**. At the very least this will include answers to coursebook exercises and a tapescript of the recorded material. Most teacher's books offer far more. For example, they may include extensive teacher's notes with suggestions for classroom management and exploitation of the material in the coursebook, additional activities, cultural background information for coursebook texts, advice on marking written work and on evaluating speaking tasks, a detailed account of the exam, end-of-unit tests, and so on. It is always a good idea to get hold of the teacher's book as this will save a lot of preparation time.

For some contexts, publishers also produce 'companions'. These are glossaries of all the vocabulary used in the coursebook, sometimes accompanied by practice exercises catering for the needs of speakers of a particular first language. Even if a companion is not available for the country concerned, it may be worth getting hold of a copy of a companion written for students elsewhere because many offer interesting and useful exercises that can be assigned to 'early-finishers' or to the whole class.

Increasingly, exam coursebooks are accompanied by **workbooks**. Workbooks usually come in two versions: one with the answer key included in the middle or at the end of the book and another in which there is no key. Some offer only grammar and vocabulary practice to supplement the coursebook; others include grammar summaries, skills work, advice on exam strategies and procedures, learner training, and practice test material. If the workbook covers all four skills, it will also be accompanied by audiocassettes of recorded material and/or a CD. In the case of CDs, these are sometimes given away free with the workbook. It is worth checking to see if the publisher has produced a 'country-specific' version of the workbook. Like the companions, these offer extra exercises, and sometimes tests, covering the specific problem areas for a particular group of speakers.

A recent innovation is to produce coursebook material for one exam board and to accompany it with two types of workbook: one catering for the same exam board as the coursebook and the other for another exam board with a test at a corresponding level. For example, the coursebook might be geared to Cambridge ESOL FCE but at the same time offer good preparation for students planning to take Michigan ECCE. The coursebook will therefore be accompanied by a choice of workbooks offering specific exam practice: one for FCE and the other for ECCE (see, for example, the Longman *Gold* series).

Some publishers now offer electronic – **online** or **CD-ROM** – versions of their exam courses. These may be intended to supplement or replace print materials. They usually include additional exercises specifically written for the medium. There is a tendency for courses to be accompanied by a **video**, intended to provide stimuli and input for the writing paper of certain exams.

The **time factor** will again be an important part of planning. How long it will take to cover the material depends on how many components there are and how many the teacher intends to use. It is worth noting that the vast majority of coursebooks are free-standing and when the publishers refer to the number of hours it takes to cover the course they are usually referring to the coursebook on its own. Many coursebooks are organized in terms of longer units which might take as long as fifteen hours to complete. Others are divided into much shorter units that can be readily covered in two or three two-hour classes. The number of units in a coursebook varies considerably as well. Obviously, assigning a workbook, CD-ROM, or other additional component adds more hours to the course planned, and it is important to decide how feasible this is and whether students would need to cover all or just some of the exercises.

Materials appropriate for use outside a class

Some workbooks can be used by students preparing for an exam independently of a class, either entirely on their own or with a private tutor. **Exam handbooks** also offer what is primarily intended as self-study material, though they can, of course, also be used in class. As the name suggests, they are very much geared to the particular exam concerned and offer exam-targeted practice, tips, hints, and exam procedures. Unlike workbooks and coursebooks, the material in the handbook will not always be graded, and they will also give less space to language development per se. Since they are aimed at the independent learner, they normally include exercises that can be corrected from the answer key (usually found at the back of the book). Handbooks generally come with either cassettes or CDs including examples of speaking tasks and listening material.

Many **CD-ROMs** can be used on their own or with minimal input from a teacher. The materials are generally at least partially interactive in that they will 'mark' the answers that a learner provides. They may also provide hints and/or reference material that students can access if they have difficulty answering or get an answer wrong. Sometimes the material will include an *avatar* (a computer-animated character) who provides feedback through sound file recordings of encouraging comments.

There are now **online versions** of several major exam courses and banks of exam practice exercises written by staff at major language schools. In the case of the material produced by language schools, there is sometimes the opportunity for students to pay for email tutorials and to send in written work for comment and correction. One particularly innovative site (Flo-Joe) offers a service where student written work is corrected and annotated and then published on the net for others to see. Some sites make extensive use of audio files and offer good listening materials and remedial pronunciation work. Chat and discussion forums are an important element on some sites, and there are even online courses that use meeting software so that students may actually participate in speaking practice either with a tutor or with other students. A few sites are free or offer some free services, usually as an enticement to get people to sign up for the fee-paying elements. Once a subscription or fee has been paid, in many cases there is almost unlimited access to practice materials.

Supplementary materials

- **Dictionaries and grammars** – several publishers recommend a particular dictionary, or sometimes a grammar, as companion volumes to their exam courses. There are usually activities in the coursebook and workbook that encourage students to learn to exploit dictionaries, though cross-referencing to a grammar is rarer, largely because most coursebooks include their own grammar reference.

  Obviously buying a coursebook and a workbook, plus a dictionary, and/or a grammar represents a considerable outlay for any student and may be very expensive. That said, a monolingual learner's dictionary is always a good investment, as is a reference grammar with exercises. If plenty of time is available and the teacher has course design expertise, it might even be possible to ask students to buy only a dictionary and a grammar. The rest of the tasks can be prepared by the teacher and, in some cases, by the students themselves.

  There are now online versions of most of the major learners' dictionaries and electronic (usually CD-ROM) versions of many good grammars aimed at intermediate level and above.

- **Practice test books** – although some recently published practice test books (and a CD-ROM) include exam tips and advice, traditionally these have contained only materials reflecting the level and content of the exam itself. In some cases, the tests are actual past papers. A typical book would contain between three and five tests presented in identical format to the exam, with an answer key. In the case of exams that include a speaking and/or a listening test, the practice test book will be accompanied by an audio cassette or CD.

  Unadulterated practice tests can be used to best effect with students in two contexts: at the beginning and at the end of the course. At the start of the course, a confident group of students can be assigned tasks from practice tests or past papers to give them a 'feel' for the level and nature of the exam. It is probably best simply to provide students with the answer key and get them to mark their own work, reminding them that they have a course of preparation ahead of them and thus should not worry unduly if they do not score well. It is sometimes necessary to use practice tests to discourage a student who is too far below the required level from registering for the exam. Exam registration is generally very expensive and it is best to deter someone who is not ready; a poor result on a practice test is often an effective means of doing this.

At the end of the course, practice tests can be used to give students experience of what it will be like to do. the exam itself and can be administered under exam conditions (or a close approximation). This can serve to alleviate anxiety and, if preparation has been well-handled, to raise confidence. The teacher can go through the answers and use this as the basis for revision, revisiting relevant sections of the coursebook or workbook to review problematic areas of grammar, vocabulary, or exam technique.

Practice test materials can also be adapted in various ways, and students can even be asked to do this for their classmates. A listening passage can be used with a simplified task, or with a reading text accompanied by a glossary, or to practise guessing meaning from context. Reading texts can also be adapted for use as gap fills to practise a particular grammar point or to further develop knowledge of vocabulary. Speaking materials probably lend themselves most readily to teaching rather than testing. Images can be used as the basis for class or group discussion.

Although teachers should be encouraged to try adapting the texts and images in practice tests for teaching purposes, it is not generally advisable to adapt them for other kinds of testing. If a reading passage is accompanied by a particular reading task, e.g. multiple matching, it is highly unlikely that the text will be suitable for another task type, e.g. gapped text. Likewise, a listening passage intended for a note-taking task will not generally work well with true/false questions.

Teacher-generated course materials

Many teachers – including exam teachers – enjoy producing their own materials. Time limitations are one of the main obstacles to generating tailored courses. Teachers who have not yet tried materials writing will find that this book offers ideas and guidance. When producing our own materials, it is essential to check that what we write accurately reflects the demands of the exams that our students are taking.'

Most teachers build up files of interesting texts to exploit as reading, grammar, and vocabulary practice material. Nowadays, with so much text available online and with the possibility of searching for particular topic areas, rather than combing the daily press, many of us can find texts for adaptation and exploitation very readily on the Internet. Listening material can be recorded from radio and TV, but web-based sound files can also be used. Since it is possible to download images, it is also far easier than it once was to prepare attractive speaking materials. Teachers should inform themselves of possible restrictions with regard to recording, copying, reproducing, and distributing copyright material from electronic and print sources, and seek any necessary permissions.

One source of text and talk that is often neglected is the students themselves. Higher-level student writing (with the originating student's permission, of course) can be used as reading material at lower levels, and recordings of speaking tasks to practise listening.

Students also enjoy and benefit from writing their own materials, either for their classmates or for students in lower-level classes. They may, for example, prepare cloze passages or reading tasks, particularly scrambled or gapped-text tasks. They can either use texts they find on the Internet or alternatively exploit texts they have written themselves. They can be asked to give short talks in class and to prepare true/false or gap-fill questions to test their classmates' listening comprehension. Students will also probably enjoy looking for images in magazines or on the Internet to use as a basis for speaking work. Throughout this book are a number of other suggestions about how the students' creative energy can be tapped in the preparation of materials. Teachers might like to try some of these out, even if they have not involved students in this way before.

An extremely important teacher factor that affects course planning decisions is the amount of time we have available. Although we may endeavour to be creative, as teachers, we should not feel guilty or inadequate if we only use published materials. The exam courses that are produced by the commercial publishers involve huge investment in terms of research, author selection, piloting, and reporting by teachers and examiners. They should, as a result, be able to provide us and our students with pretty much everything necessary for exam preparation and can guarantee that what is provided reflects the exam concerned as accurately as possible. Especially if we teach more than twenty hours a week, using a published exam course still remains our best option.

Conclusions   In this chapter we have:
- examined the factors to consider when planning an exam course.
- provided an example of a class profile and a planning scenario.
- discussed the way in which class size affects decisions about approach.
- looked at the effect of age on choice of methodology and materials.
- examined a variety of learning contexts and their impact on course planning.
- noted that there may be linguistic and cultural factors to take into account.
- discussed the impact of time limitations.
- considered classes in which not all students are taking the exam, and also how to support students who have not taken an exam before.
- provided an overview of available exam course materials for use in, or outside, a class situation.
- explored a range of considerations when choosing materials.
- explained the circumstances in which the use of practice tests is appropriate.
- considered how and when materials might usefully be generated by the teacher and students themselves.

How to teach reading for exams

- **The different types of reading test**
- **What is measured in reading tests**
- **How to prepare students for reading tests**
- **Exam procedures and strategies for students**

Students have usually had plenty of reading practice before they begin an exam course but this does not necessarily imply that they have had sufficient practice of exam-specific skills. Even in exam coursebooks, not all reading sections are particularly geared towards engendering these skills. Although non-exam reading activities provide valuable practice of reading skills per se, students should aim to be familiar and confident with the tasks that occur in the exam they are taking, and with the procedures to be followed when tackling these tasks.

The different types of reading test

The reading component in most exams reflects the wide range of purposes for which people read in real life. Typical reading exams include texts of different types and lengths. Increasingly, the texts used are authentic or semi-authentic (drawn from magazines, newspapers etc) – texts written for competent or native speakers of English, rather than being written specifically for teaching or testing. The texts are accompanied by a variety of reading tasks, each of which is designed to test a particular combination of reading skills. The following are the most common tasks.

Multiple choice

This is the reading task that is likely to be most familiar to students. It consists of a text (or texts), which can be of almost any type (narrative, argument, descriptive etc) and genre (stories, letters, articles, signs etc), accompanied by one or more multiple choice items (where students have to choose between alternatives, e.g. a, b, c, or d). These may be in the form of a series of statements, a question plus answers, or an incomplete statement with a choice of phrases or words with which to complete it. There are usually three or four options, only one of which is correct. It is common to have items corresponding to specific sections of the text, but there may also be items to test comprehension of the text as a whole.

True/false

This is another task type that will be familiar to most students. Once again, there is a text or a group of texts accompanied by a series of statements. Candidates determine whether the statements are correct (true) or incorrect (false), according to the text. Sometimes a third option is included ('not given' or 'not known'), for cases where the text does not give the reader enough information to determine whether a statement is true or false. A variant on this task is simply to ask questions, to be answered 'yes' or 'no', about the subject matter dealt with in the text.

Matching

Less familiar perhaps, but increasingly common, are matching tasks. They are used by several of the exam boards, some of which include more than one matching task in their reading tests.

In matching tasks, candidates choose from a list of prompts. The prompts may be headings, statements, or question completions. For example, candidates might be asked to match a description to the appropriate paragraph of a text, or to match words and phrases to their meanings. The texts used are frequently descriptive, but can be from a range of genres (book reviews, biographies, travel guides, articles etc). Sometimes there is a single text divided into sections and on other occasions a series of short, related texts is used.

Low-level and young learners' reading tests make liberal use of matching tasks, because visuals can be used as well as short texts, such as notices or signs.

Gapped texts

Tasks involving texts (including text in charts and diagrams) from which single words, phrases, sentences, or paragraphs have been removed are also common to many reading tests. Single word, phrase, or sentence gap fills are found in tests of grammar and vocabulary too (see Chapter 5).

In some tasks, it is the candidates who have to decide what should fill the gap, while in others they must choose (as with multiple choice tasks) from a series of alternatives, only one of which is correct. Where paragraphs or sentences have been removed, there is usually an item among the alternatives that does not belong to the text.

In some cases, the candidate writes in the words or figures that are missing from a diagram, summary, or chart that accompanies the main text. For the most part, however, in this type of task only single texts are used. These are of many types, but descriptive narratives are particularly frequent. They can be drawn from fiction, biography, articles, or letters.

Gapped texts provide a task type that lends itself to the use of visual materials, and so can be found in reading tests for younger learners. This kind of task may also be applied to dialogues in lower-level exams.

Proofreading

Proofreading tasks involve finding deliberate errors of various kinds in the text provided. Although they typically form a part of grammar and vocabulary tests, proofreading tasks are also used by some exam boards in reading exams.

The texts can be of any type and genre, though they are usually shorter than texts used in other parts of the reading test. In most cases, each line of the text is numbered. Some lines will contain an extra word, a misspelt word, or a punctuation error, while other lines will be correct. Candidates are required to read the text and mark lines as correct, or locate the extra words, or correct the spelling and punctuation errors.

What is measured in reading tests

Some exams test reading and writing together, and candidates are expected to write longer responses to what they have read; these responses are also assessed as pieces of writing. Even where there is a separate reading test, there is often overlap between the testing of reading and the testing of writing. Many writing tests (see Chapter 4) involve quite a lot of reading. The same is true for tests of 'English in Use', which, although they focus primarily on grammar and vocabulary (see Chapter 5), are frequently text-based and so test reading sub-skills. Students need to be aware of this as they sometimes do poorly in the writing or use of English section of an exam because of limitations in their reading ability.

Each of the parts in a typical reading test is designed to measure a different combination of reading skills. Lower-level tests measure candidates' ability to understand the main message and some detail. Only short factual texts (e.g. notices and letters) are used. At intermediate level and above, students are expected to be able to handle a full range of text types and genres, and text lengths of over a thousand words. More advanced tests are designed to measure a greater range of reading skills. Below and on the next pages are a list of the reading skills tested in exam tasks, each with an example test item and a brief explanation of how the task is typically used.

Understanding the main ideas
- multiple choice
- matching

What is the writer complaining about in the letter?

A Buses are becoming more crowded.
B Bus stops are poorly maintained.
C Adults can be thoughtless on buses.
D Children should be more polite on buses.

The skill here is reading for gist or skimming. The candidate needs to read the text (in the example above, a letter) through from beginning to end. It is not normally possible to find any single, small section of the text that provides the answer to the question. Instead, the answer is derived from understanding whole paragraphs or the entire text.

Finding specific information and detail
- multiple choice
- matching

> **Look at the eight recruitment advertisements (A–H). Answer the questions below by writing the letters of the appropriate advertisements A–H in boxes 1–10 on your answer sheet.**
>
> 1 Which TWO positions require a knowledge of computers?
> 2 Which position is for only a temporary appointment? ... etc.

In this case, the reading sub-skill to be used is scanning, i.e. looking through the whole text to locate key words and phrases. Generally, the words and phrases used in the questions do not occur in the text or texts, so students need to be able to recognize synonyms and parallel expressions, or, in the case of visuals, to activate the vocabulary related to the visuals and locate it in the text.

Recognizing the writer's attitude and opinion
- multiple choice

> **The writer thinks that companies who advertise on the Internet**
>
> A try to exploit their customers.
> B should be more carefully monitored.
> C are more common in the the United States.
> D never sell quality products.

The answer will not usually be stated explicitly at any one point in the text. An appreciation of the writer's attitude or opinion depends on picking up the meaning of adverbs and modal expressions that may be scattered throughout the text.

Identifying the tone
- multiple choice

> **The writer's comments on the new exhibition centre are**
>
> A admiring.
> B critical.
> C mildly complimentary.
> D slightly dismissive.

Once again, we generally appreciate a particular tone on the basis of evidence found in many parts of the text, rather than in a single sentence or paragraph. Modal verbs, adverbs, and adjectives throughout the text will contribute to our seeing the tone as critical, admiring etc.

Understanding implication

- multiple choice

The author implies that male nurses

A are unprofessional.
B have been undervalued.
C do not take their work seriously.
D cannot compete with their female counterparts.

Here it is necessary to 'read between the lines' and understand what is not said overtly, rather than looking for the answer somewhere in the words of the text themselves. For example, if I ask you if you like your job and you answer that it is, at least, well paid, I can infer that the money is probably the only good thing about it, in your view. It is also important to distinguish between what the text actually implies and one's own ideas and beliefs.

Identifying the purpose for which the text was written

- multiple choice

What would be the best title for this text?

A How to get along with people in the office
B My first day at work
C Why you shouldn't work with your relatives
D The diary of a copywriter

Once again, there will not necessarily be any one section of the text in which the purpose is stated, though sometimes grammar will be a good indicator. A story primarily intended to entertain will, in all likelihood, be told using narrative tenses (simple past, past continuous, past perfect) whereas if the intention is to advise, we would expect to find structures such as imperatives and modals of obligation (*should, ought to, must, have to*).

Understanding text structure and organization

- gapped text
- proofreading

[See the example on page 32.]

Text pattern recognition skills are brought to bear in scrambled text activities, so most students will have already had plenty of practice when using general English reading materials. There are a number of different patterns that students need to learn to recognize. For example, in *narratives*, sections of the text will introduce characters and setting, and there will be a series of events or actions that create some kind of problem that is then resolved in some way. In *description*, there is frequently a transition from the general to the particular, while in *discursive texts* a common pattern involves

> **Choose the most suitable sentence from the list (a–f) for each gap (1–6) in the article.**

a) Macy says she wants to know about her past even if it is very frightening.

b) Walking around a lake made her feel that she had always liked being outside in the fresh air.

c) This illness can be caused by a head injury to the brain or by a shocking event.

d) She told the operator she didn't know where she was – or who she was.

e) There was no wallet and nothing to identify her.

f) Everything before March 2 is completely blank.

The woman with no name

It's as if Macy's life began two weeks ago. She found herself alone and shivering from the cold on the side of a completely unfamiliar road.

She remembers feeling a bump on the back of her head and looking in the pockets of her jeans and long brown coat. She found $24.31 and a pink cigarette lighter. That was all she found. (1) ....e......... .

It was just after midnight on March 2nd when she went into a phone box outside a petrol station near a small town in Virginia, USA and dialled the emergency number 911. (2) ....d........ . She can't recall how long she walked that night and she can't remember anything else.

Macy has a classic case of amnesia. (3) .... She has no memories of friends or family and no memories of playing with classmates as a child. She doesn't know if she is a wife or a mother or if she has a favourite colour. She doesn't remember any films, books, names, faces or places. She didn't recognise the President of the United States when she saw him on television or remember any recent events.

Medical experts say cases like Macy's, in which there is such a complete loss of memory, are quite rare. (4) .... Usually the effects do not last long and the period of time that the person has forgotten is normally limited.

Macy's doctors said medical tests show that she is healthy. They think something really terrible might have happened to her and that this made her mind cut off all her memories. (5) ....

Macy has noticed some things that seem familiar. A desire to paint her nails pink made her think she might have enjoyed doing that before. (6) .... She can't explain why she chose the name Macy, but wonders if it has something to do with her past.

Macy's doctors say all she can do is wait. She says she is also praying, although she doesn't even know if she has ever done that before.

Extracts on pages 32 and 33 adapted from:
Going for Gold – Intermediate Maximiser by Sally Burgess (Longman)

introducing a problem and then offering a series of possible solutions, each of which is evaluated. Students also need to appreciate that individual paragraphs contain topic sentences, while other sentences in the paragraph support the topic sentence by providing detail, examples, and so on.

Understanding cohesion and coherence

- gapped text
- proofreading
- multiple choice

> a) Macy says she wants to know about her past even if it is very frightening.
>
> b) Walking around a lake made her feel that she had always liked being outside in the fresh air.
>
> c) This illness can be caused by a head injury to the brain or by a shocking event.
>
> d) She told the operator she didn't know where she was – or who she was.
>
> e) There was no wallet and nothing to identify her.
>
> f) Everything before March 2 is completely blank.

> Macy has a classic case of amnesia. (3) .... She has no memories of friends or family and no memories of playing with classmates as a child. She doesn't know if she is a wife

Cohesion is a quality of texts such that elements (words, clauses, sentences, and paragraphs) are connected to one another. Coherence is the logical connection between ideas and concepts in a text. One way in which readers understand text organization is by looking for such relationships at the level of individual words and phrases. This may involve understanding the meanings of pronouns (in the example above, *Macy says she wants to know about her past even if it is very frightening.*). Or, it can involve understanding that the use of a definite article or a demonstrative adjective (e.g. *this*) can indicate that something has been mentioned earlier in the text (*Macy has a classic case of **amnesia** ... **This illness** can be caused by a head injury*), or that there is a relationship between lexical items, i.e. that they are synonyms, opposites, parts of a whole, and so on. In gapped-text tasks, students can check their intuitive guesses about the position of sentences and paragraphs by looking for these relationships. Students may be asked about the meaning of a pronoun or determiner plus a general noun (e.g. *this illness*) in some multiple choice tests.

Understanding the meaning of specific words in context

- gapped text
- matching
- multiple choice

> **The word _crestfallen_ in line 31 is closest in meaning to:**
>
> **A** irritated
> **B** relieved
> **C** disappointed
> **D** proud

This is not a question of how much vocabulary students know, but of their being able to work out the meaning of unfamiliar items from context. This generally involves looking at the immediate environment in which the word or phrase occurs and sometimes for clues in terms of the form of the word, e.g. negative prefixes.

There are many ways in which teachers can support students in developing the skills measured in reading tests, but it is important to highlight the connection between particular reading activities and the demands of the exam. For example, when presenting a scrambled text activity (i.e. a text in which the order of sentences or paragraphs has been changed), the benefit will be greater if the teacher explains how this helps students to prepare for gapped-text tasks.

How to prepare students for reading tests

Teachers do not always feel comfortable about devoting precious class time to reading, since reading tasks can conveniently be assigned as homework. While it is often reasonable to expect students to carry out reading assignments in their own time, class time can be used very profitably to work on three areas: 1) developing task awareness, 2) developing exam skills and strategies, and 3) improving reading speeds.

Developing task awareness

We can ensure that students appreciate the value of reading practice in exam classes by familiarizing them with the exam itself. Candidates need to know how many parts there are in the reading exam and what kinds of tasks occur in each part.

Good exam coursebooks or workbooks normally provide an exam overview at the beginning. It is sensible to go over this information with students at the beginning of the course. If an exam overview is not provided, teachers can prepare their own. The overview should include the following information:

- how long the reading exam lasts
- how many parts there are
- how long students have to do each part
- what tasks can occur in each part
- how to answer the questions (e.g. choose between the alternatives)
- how long the texts are in each part
- how many words students have to read overall

Because so many reading exams involve entering answers on a sheet that can be read by a computer, it is important to make sure that students know how to fill these sheets in.

The details of each task and the kinds of items that occur are best introduced gradually as the course progresses. Each part of the exam should be covered at least once, if not more often. Ideally, there will be enough exam reading practice in the course to engage all the reading skills that are tested by each task.

Teachers can provide information about the tasks used, explain what kinds of reading they are designed to test, and suggest procedures for tackling them. Specific strategies for each task can also be presented and demonstrated. This can be accompanied by an example of the particular task, so that students can try out the procedure and put the strategy into practice. They should then have further practice with the procedure at a later point in the course.

Developing exam skills and strategies

Unless the course is an intensive one in which students have only a very short time to prepare for the exam, it is best to use graded materials. Tasks, texts, and the conditions in which students read will become increasingly 'exam-authentic' – focused on exams themselves rather than on authentic reading in general – as we move closer to the exam date. This approach is more motivating because students will have a good chance of getting many of the answers right, even at the beginning of the course. Exam reading preparation can be graded in three ways: 1) by simplifying the tasks, 2) by simplifying the texts, and 3) by gradually introducing students to exam conditions.

Simplifying the task

Reading tasks can be simplified in a number of ways, according to the task type. Here are some methods:

- include fewer questions.
- include only those questions that measure a particular skill, e.g. only attitude and opinion questions.
- include fewer distractors, e.g. fewer options in multiple choice, no extra paragraph/sentence with a gapped text (that is, the number of paragraphs/sentences offered for matching would be the same as the number of gaps), all lines of text incorrect in proofreading (normally, there are several lines of text that do not contain errors).
- avoid distracting ambiguity, e.g. no 'overlap' between matches in multiple matching (where headings are matched to paragraphs or sections of text). In tests, there are often one or two headings that might seem to apply to several sections/paragraphs. To simplify the task, we can make the headings clear-cut summaries of topic sentences (while still avoiding using the same words).
- include only distractors offering opportunities to practise a particular exam strategy, e.g. multiple choice options which say something that is true but not mentioned in the text.

- provide (some) answers and indicate why they are right/wrong.
- highlight parts of the text where answers are to be found.

Simplifying tasks is relatively straightforward. Material from past papers or texts from practice exams books can be modified for use, and many exam coursebooks include simplified tasks.

Simplifying the text

Another aspect of the gradual process of developing exam reading skills and strategies involves applying those skills and strategies to increasingly complex texts. This means that students only meet texts at the level of the exam itself when they are thoroughly familiar with the task procedures and have a good grasp of exam reading strategies.

The following are points to consider when selecting or simplifying texts for exam classes:

- **Length** – many interesting magazine and newspaper articles and most short stories are simply too long for classroom use, though they may, of course, be assigned for extensive reading (i.e. reading for information or pleasure, usually without structured comprehension questions). For use in class, authentic texts like these will need to be edited. In the case of news stories, this is relatively straightforward, as one can generally edit from the bottom up, cutting paragraphs until the required length is reached. Other texts can present more of a challenge; one approach is to read the text a couple of times, put it aside and then write a summary of the length the students can manage (how faithful the short version is to the flavour of the original will depend on the teacher).
- **Number of unknown words** – we usually develop good intuitions about words that will present difficulties for students and can therefore edit the text so that there are not too many of them. If teaching in a context where we do not speak the students' first language, or in a multilingual context, we might try giving any texts we are thinking of using to students at the level above the level of the class with which we are planning to use the text. We can ask these more advanced students to highlight all the words they know. We are then left with the unknown words. We can edit these out to ensure that every sentence contains enough familiar words to allow our learners to work out meaning from context.
- **Number of unfamiliar structures** (e.g. participle clauses, such as, *Feeling extremely anxious, I phoned to say I couldn't go.*) – a grammar syllabus (shown, for example, on the contents page of a coursebook) should indicate which structures are being revised, and which are presented and practised for the first time. Ideally, the text should not include too high a proportion of grammar the students have not yet met. If it does, it should probably be simplified. This is particularly important where there is also unfamiliar vocabulary.
- **How much is left implicit** – if the text is complex in terms of grammar and vocabulary, we may decide to make explicit what has been left implicit in the original text. The summary writing technique suggested above may help here, in that we may find that in our summary we have actually expressed what the original text simply implied.

- **How much background knowledge is needed** – students generally enjoy reading texts from which they can learn something new, but can be bewildered and irritated by texts that assume that the reader too grew up where the author did. This applies particularly to humour. Texts that may have teachers rolling on the floor with laughter will often leave their students cold. We can remove or modify references to particular times, people, and places, but if too much cultural or specialist background knowledge is required to achieve an understanding of a text, it is probably safest to reject it.
- **How clear is the text structure** – we might expect a text written by a professional to be exemplary in terms of text structure, but this is not always the case. Sometimes a lot is left up to the reader and the teacher will need to make relationships between sections of the text more explicit. For example, if there is a cause and effect relationship that may not be clear to students, we could introduce a rhetorical question, e.g. *Why do people do this? One reason is that* … . We might even add a line or two to make these links clearer.
- **How likely it is that the topic will come up in the exam** – students will want practice with the vocabulary and background knowledge needed to tackle exam text topics, but they may also enjoy reading texts with content and style that are not likely to come up in the exam. Many topics that exam boards deem too controversial for use in their tests may still be appropriate for classroom use.

Simplification is useful and necessary, particularly early in an exam course, but it is important not to go too far in this respect. Students need to get a feel for texts at the level of complexity they will meet in the exam. It is important to preserve as much as possible of the original text so as to give learners access to the kinds of authentic texts they need to read for exam and non-exam purposes.

Gradually introducing exam conditions

The conditions under which students do reading tasks in class can gradually approximate to those of the exam room. Early in the course, students can be encouraged to discuss their answers in pairs or groups, before offering them to the whole class. Students may also be asked to do some reading tasks outside class, especially if they have a workbook as well as a coursebook. This usually means that they can spend as much time on the task as they wish and that they may use dictionaries to check meaning. Even in class we might pre-teach some of the vocabulary in the text. As we progress through the course, these 'cushions' may gradually be eliminated so that eventually most reading will be done under conditions like those in the exam. This means that (if feasible):

- it will be timed
- students will work individually
- no guidance will be given about how to approach the task
- dictionaries etc. cannot be used
- answers will be entered on a facsimile of the answer sheet

Improving reading speeds

Even those students with good reading speeds in their first language, or who read extensively for non-exam purposes, may have difficulty with timing in reading exams. It can sometimes be hard to convince students of this, however.

It is essential that they know how much they have to read and how much time they have to do it in. We can make students aware of time limitations at the beginning of the course by asking them to read a text of the maximum length required in the exam and do the accompanying task. When the time that would be allocated to this task in the exam is up, their answers are collected, regardless of whether they have finished answering the questions or not. They may well be frustrated, but the point will have been made.

After this, it is useful always to set time limits and stick to them, while initially allowing slightly more time than candidates will have in the exam. The teacher can bring an alarm clock or a timer to class, and warn students five minutes before their task time is up. Encouraging students to keep an eye on the clock or timer, those who finish within the allotted time can be rewarded by having their name entered on a record of 'speedy readers'. This means that everyone can finish their reading but that those who go over time are fully aware of this because they are not put on the 'speedy readers' list. Students can also be encouraged to take over the role of time keeper, timing a partner and then themselves without the teacher's intervention.

An important factor in reading speeds is how students cope when they encounter unfamiliar vocabulary in a text. Slow readers get stuck on individual words, while fluent, faster readers are more concerned with meaning beyond the sentence and do not hesitate even if there is quite a high proportion of new vocabulary. We can help students by teaching them to:

* distinguish between essential and non-essential words
* work out meaning from context
* work out meaning from word form

One way of getting students to see just how much meaning one can derive from context, and how much redundancy there is in most texts, is to give them a familiar reading passage in a language they do not know at all (but with some relationship to their first language or to English), e.g. *Little Red Riding Hood* in Esperanto. Once they have worked out the meaning of the title and the first line, they will often be able to 'read' the story without 'knowing' any of the words.

Here is a lower-intermediate level sample lesson which helps learners look systematically at working out meaning from context.

Example lesson

The students are asked to do a reading task in which the text contains from five to ten words or expressions that will be unfamiliar to them. They are asked to tell a partner what they normally do when they find a word they don't understand. The teacher then distributes this sheet with students' techniques and asks if the pairs mentioned any of these:

> **A** I continue reading and try not to worry about the words I don't understand.
> **B** I look all the words up in a dictionary.
> **C** I look up important words in my dictionary.
> **D** I try and work out the meaning of important words from the context.

Students can be asked to match these strategies to some comments by other students (these can be printed on the reverse side of the sheet):

> **1** 'This doesn't work. Some words are not important and it takes much too long to read the text!'
> **2** 'This is a very good idea. When you work out the meaning from context you usually remember the new word better.'
> **3** 'This is not such a good idea. You might not understand anything at all!'
> **4** 'This can be very useful but I only do it when I've already tried to work out what the word means from context.'

The teacher then writes on the board:

> The cat was sleeping peacefully in his favourite spot on the Chesterfield. I sat down next to him.

The class is asked how they work out the meaning (of *Chesterfield*, which is almost certain to be the unknown word) from the context. Using this example, these steps are elicited:

- Decide on the part of speech (noun, verb, adjective etc) of the word.
- Look at the words and sentences before and after the word.
- Try to think of another word (including a word in a better-known language or a general word) that could replace the unknown word.

This leads to the next exercise (or a similar one of the teacher's own).

Firstly, the students study the activity on page 40 and are asked to say what part of speech the nonsense words are. This can be done in open class. Then students work individually on deciding the meaning before checking their answers with a partner and then in open class.

Students finally go back to the reading text which they studied at the beginning of the lesson and try to work out the meaning of the words or expressions that were new to them. The teacher can either say which words or expressions students should work on or ask them to choose their own. If they have worked on words of their own choosing, they can then teach a partner these new words and expressions.

> **Look at the words in italics in these sentences (they are not real English words!). Decide what they mean by looking at the words and sentences before and after them. Underline the words that help you decide. The first one has been done for you as an example.**
>
> 0 A <u>bright red</u> *gimble* came round the corner very fast and almost <u>knocked me down</u>. <u>The driver</u> didn't even see me.
>
>   A *gimble* is: A a type of car
>
>   B a type of animal
>
> 1 She *nordled* all her final exams because she hadn't studied at all.
>
>   To *nordle* means: A to sing   B to fail
>
> 2 He was wearing jeans, a t-shirt and a pair of *galvies*.
>
>   *Galvies* are: A shoes   B books
>
> 3 Francesca is a very *snorpy* person. Terrible things are always happening to her.
>
>   *Snorpy* means: A unlucky   B lucky
>
> 4 She *toogled* into the classroom and told everyone the news.
>
>   To *toogle* means: A to smile   B to run

Adapted from:
Going for Gold – Intermediate Maximiser
by Sally Burgess (Longman)

Exam procedures and strategies for students

In addition to developing their overall reading skills and familiarity with the tasks they will meet, students also need to become well-versed in a series of exam procedures and strategies. There are several procedures and strategies that apply to all exam tasks, while others are applicable to a specific task type.

Time management

Typical reading tests last between an hour and an hour and a half. In most cases, any one part of the test is expected to take roughly the same amount of time to complete as any other, though some tests (e.g. IELTS) include texts and tasks of increasing difficulty. Students need to learn how to allocate their time so that they do not spend too long on one part of the test and then run short of time for the other parts. They also need to allow time for entering their answers on an answer sheet that is, in many cases, marked electronically.

General procedures and strategies

Students should use the following procedures in all reading tasks:

- Look at the title and try to **predict** what they will read about.
- **Skim** the text(s) to get a general idea of meaning.
- **Read the test items** only after they have skimmed the text.
- **Use specific procedures** (see page 41) to choose their answers.
- Where possible, identify specific parts of the text that **justify answers.**
- **Go on to the next question** even if they are not sure of the answer to the previous one.

Research into reading shows that by looking at the title we activate background knowledge we already hold and are able to make certain predictions about what we are going to read. Having done this, we read to confirm or refute our predictions and are less likely to be slowed down or totally confounded by unfamiliar words or structures.

Students can be trained to look at text titles and to make predictions. In the early stages of the course they might, for example, be asked to speculate about the relationships between the title and the images accompanying a text. Even if there is no visual material, they can look at the title and suggest what they think the text is going to be about and what kind of text they expect it to be (e.g. giving advice or telling a story). Trying to predict the content from the title provides a good lead-in to skimming the text, as in the following activity.

Example lesson

Given a titled piece of text, students read it quickly to check their predictions (made first on the basis of the title alone). We can ensure that they do not get bogged down at this point by setting a strict time limit. It can be made clear that there will be an opportunity to read the text more carefully later.

Once students have read the text through quickly, they can look at the questions (also provided). They will often find that they can readily answer some of these and should be encouraged to do so. Even if they are not certain of any answers, they will now be in a much better position to identify the parts of the text where the answers are to be found, so their second reading will be much more focused and, therefore, more efficient.

As they read the text for the second time, students should carefully check any answers they have already decided on, and find answers to the other questions. They should be encouraged to underline or highlight the relevant parts of the text. In the early stages of the course some or all of the underlining can be done for them. The lines in texts in exam coursebooks are usually numbered and the teacher's book usually indicates where the answers are to be found. When checking through at the end of the reading task, the teacher can insist that students justify their answers by referring to the text.

Specific procedures and strategies

Whatever the type of reading task, students should begin by following the general procedures just described, that is, trying to predict what the text will be about on the basis of the title and skimming to get a general idea of meaning. Then – and only then – should they decide on their answers using specific strategies suited to each type of task.

Multiple choice

1 Read the text again carefully.
2 Look at the multiple choice questions one by one, without looking at the options, and try to answer them in your own words.
3 Look at the alternatives and see which is closest to your own version.
4 Check that the other alternatives are wrong (if there is time).

Matching tasks

1 Look at the prompts one at a time and scan the text(s) to find the answer.
2 Underline 'parallel expressions' (i.e. expressions with similar meanings in the text(s) and prompts).

Gapped text

1 Read the base text carefully, focusing on the sentences (or words) either side of the gap.
2 Try to fill in gaps in your own words.
3 Look at full nouns, pronouns, possessive adjectives (*her*, *their* etc), and determiners (*the*, *that* etc) in both the base text and the sentences/paragraphs and try to work out what they refer back or forward to.
4 Decide on a sentence or paragraph for each gap.
5 Double check if you find you want to use the same sentence or paragraph twice.

Proofreading

1 Read the text sentence by sentence to locate the errors.
2 Put a tick at the end of correct lines.
3 Put the correction at the end of the incorrect lines.
4 Make sure that you have located and corrected errors in only some of the lines in the text (exam boards usually stipulate a maximum number of lines with errors).

The final step in the procedure in each case is **entering answers on the answer sheet**. Candidates should learn either to do this as they answer or to allow time for it at the end.

Students can be introduced to these procedures and techniques in several ways. Here are some ideas for teachers:

 Do a reading task with them and ask them to suggest procedures and strategies themselves.

 Provide a jumbled list including both sensible strategies and slightly silly ones (e.g. writing the letters A, B, C, and D on the sides of a match box and then throwing it to decide your answers).

 Introduce a sequence of strategies in a jumbled order and ask students to put them into a proper order of sequence.

 Explain a procedure and strategies for a particular task type to the students and then ask them to apply them to a reading task, and evaluate their usefulness.

A final word should be said about how to avoid getting stuck on individual questions. Students should know that they cannot lose marks for incorrect answers (rather, marks are lost for failing to supply the correct answers) and that they should not leave a question unanswered. If they have trouble with a particular question, they should press on and try to come back to that question later. If they don't have time at the end to work out the answer, they should guess!

Conclusions   In this chapter we have:
- looked at the most common reading task types used in exams.
- listed the specific reading skills measured in exams.
- provided examples of questions testing each of these skills.
- indicated how students can be informed and motivated to approach exam reading.
- shown how a graded exam reading course might be designed.
- provided some considerations for simplifying reading texts.
- shown how students can gradually be familiarized with exam conditions.
- emphasized the need for reading speeds to be improved.
- discussed how students can deal with unfamiliar vocabulary in texts.
- looked at general reading procedures and strategies for all tasks.
- provided specific procedures and strategies for specific tasks, and suggested ways to introduce students to these.

How to teach writing for exams

- Writing tests compared
- What kinds of writing tasks are there?
- What is measured in writing tests?
- Assessing written work and providing feedback
- How to help students to deal with task input
- Encouraging familiarity with genres
- How to prepare students for writing exam answers
- Handwriting and presentation

Writing tests compared

Although there is much variation, particularly between UK- and US-based exams, there are many basic features that writing tests have in common:

- The number of words candidates should write is always specified and they are expected to stick to these limits, neither writing a great deal more nor a great deal less.
- Tests frequently offer a choice of writing tasks. Nowadays, most exam boards have moved away from asking candidates to write only compositions or essays. This kind of writing is still used in some tests (e.g. TOEFL) and is an option in others, but candidates are usually given a specific role and a task to perform in that role. For example, they might be asked to write a letter of complaint to the local council in the role of the representative of a neighbourhood association. The roles and tasks are intended to reflect the real-life writing needs of candidates of a certain age range and educational or professional profile.
- Even though a choice of tasks may be offered, some tests also include a compulsory task.
- Candidates usually write their answers in a booklet or on paper provided, though some boards now make provision for students to write their answer on a computer.
- The scripts are NOT marked electronically, but manually by examiners comparing them with benchmark descriptions of writing abilities within mark bands at the relevant level.

Some exam boards (e.g. Trinity, Cambridge ESOL in KET and Young Learners) test reading and writing together (see Chapter 8 on low-level exams). This is done either by including in reading tests items which involve some writing, such as gapped-text tasks, or by asking candidates to produce longer responses to reading comprehension questions and then assessing these responses as writing. Even where there is a separate writing test, there is often overlap between the testing of reading and the testing of writing. Many higher-level writing tests involve quite a lot of reading. Sometimes students do poorly in writing exams because of a failure to read and deal with the task input adequately.

There are also tasks in tests of 'English in Use' which, although they focus primarily on grammar and vocabulary (see Chapter 5), also assess writing skills by asking students to paraphrase or summarize texts.

What kinds of writing tasks are there?

Broadly speaking, exam writing tasks can be divided into three types:

- **Content and procedural knowledge-based tasks** – these are tasks that demand specific knowledge or experience of some kind (e.g. work experience in BEC and in one of the Cambridge ESOL CAE options, experience of academic study in IELTS Academic, or familiarity with set literary texts in Cambridge ESOL FCE and CPE).

- **Open-ended tasks** – in these, all content is generated by the student. Topics vary widely, but no more than common knowledge is required.

- **Input-based tasks** – here students are expected to integrate the task input into their answer. For example, a student might be asked to integrate material from notes about a job advertisement into a letter of application.

Regardless of the task type, candidates are expected to produce more than one of a wide range of **genres** (different types of writing). The following are the genres most commonly demanded in exam tasks:

- articles (magazine, newspaper)
- reports
- reviews (e.g. of films, books)
- competition entries (e.g. stories)
- leaflets and information sheets
- contributions to brochures
- applications (completion of forms and letters)
- letters (personal and formal)
- personal notes and messages
- essays (always discursive)
- compositions (these can be discursive, descriptive, or narrative)

On some occasions the answer is composed of more than one piece of writing and the candidate has to produce texts written in two or even three genres.

In almost all cases the writing tasks are unseen. The exception to this is TOEFL. A list of several hundred essay titles is published on the TOEFL website, and from this titles are chosen at random and assigned to individual candidates who do the test online.

What is measured in writing tests?

Much more is measured in writing tests than just grammatical accuracy and the amount of vocabulary the student knows (or can squeeze into an exam answer). Although students will be marked down by all exam boards for answers with grammatical and vocabulary errors that prevent them conveying the desired message, or which are regarded as below the level of the exam, grammar and vocabulary are by no means the only aspects of written communication that students need to master. Range and control of grammar and vocabulary are never assessed independently of communicative purpose. An answer that has some errors but achieves its communicative purpose will get a higher mark than an answer that is grammatically accurate but does not meet the task requirements.

Candidate scripts are marked by assessors. They examine each script and compare it to standard descriptions of candidate skills in order to arrive at a grade on a band scale. They may use descriptions of overall task achievement and/or descriptions of specific skills. Here is an example:

> **4 High Pass:** Ideas well developed, easily understood. Clearly addresses the issue. Good control of both complex and simple structures; some localized errors that do not interfere with comprehensibility. Vocabulary generally appropriate and on target.
>
> **3 Pass:** Ideas easily understood, might not be well linked. Addresses the issue. Good control of basic structures and basic vocabulary. Some complex structures and more advanced vocabulary but with errors that do not interfere with comprehensibility.
>
> From *ECCE Certificates and Scoring Procedures* on University of Michigan: English Language Institute website (http://www.lsa.umich.edu/eli)

The number of separate skills that candidates are expected to display in their writing varies according to the level of the test and how specific it is. However, it is possible to list the key skills generally measured in writing tests, and explain how these are displayed in response to exam tasks.

• **Task achievement** – in most exams the writing tasks are expressed in terms of reader and writer roles and in terms of communicative purpose, as in the following example:

> A new canteen is going to be built at your school. **The director of the school has asked you to write a report** on the things students disliked about the old canteen and what kinds of food they think should be served in the new one. You have also been asked to find out what students feel about the sale of chewing gum and cigarettes. Write a report of between 120 and 140 words.

Task achievement involves using language appropriate to the relationship between reader and writer (in the example above, the candidate is expected to use a level of formality befitting the relationship between a student and the school director) and the communicative purpose, while including material on each of the points in the task rubric. All of this has to be done within the stipulated word limit.

- **Coverage of required points** – in many exam writing tasks there is task input of some kind that candidates are expected to integrate into their answers. This may be in the form of annotations, graphs, survey results, and so on. Here is an example:

PRACTICE WRITING TEST THREE

Writing Task 1

You are advised to spend a maximum of 20 minutes on this task.

The bar chart below shows the number of overseas students enrolled in a second year Graphic Design course at a college in the south of England.

Write a report for a university lecturer describing the information shown.

You should write at least 150 words.

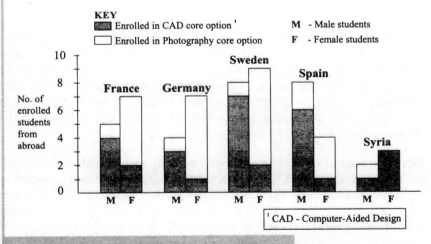

From *101 Helpful Hints for IELTS International Edition* by Garry Adams & Terry Peck (Adams & Austen Press)

- **Evidence of original output** – where there are points to cover in the task input, candidates are expected to use their own words to express them. In higher-level exams, they are also often expected to introduce some of their own ideas as well as the material specifically demanded by the rubric.

- **Range and control of structures and vocabulary** – apart from avoiding errors that prevent them achieving their communicative purpose, candidates are expected to show that they know a range of vocabulary and a variety of grammatical structures. For example, in a letter written in response to a task where candidates need to ask for various kinds of information, they would gain marks by writing a variety of question and request forms (*Could you tell me ...? I would like to know ...* etc).

- **Organization and cohesion** – candidates are expected to demonstrate an understanding of how texts are structured as a whole and of paragraph structure. This includes understanding that each paragraph contains a topic sentence and that all other sentences in the paragraph relate to that sentence. Understanding of cohesion involves showing relationships between clauses and sentences by means of linking phrases, pronouns, other **proforms** (e.g. *Most students want to use the library more often and they would **do** if it were open daily*), and the use of synonyms (e.g. *There are several **problems** with the proposed tramline. One of the **difficulties** is the cost.*), antonyms, and so on.

- **Appropriate presentation and register** – candidates need to know how the various genres (report, letter, note etc) are typically presented. They also need to use a register that is appropriate to the relationship between writer and reader, as discussed with the report to the school director (on pages 46–47).

- **Achievement of desired effect on target reader** – this involves combining an understanding of the role relationship and the communicative purpose. For example, a report written in response to the example task (at the bottom of page 46) that included a lot of very informal, colloquial language might sound presumptuous or even rude to the target reader and might cause offence. Clearly, this would not be the desired effect!

- **Development of topic** – in advanced writing exams, such as Michigan ECPE, Cambridge ESOL CPE, and IELTS, candidates are expected to do more than simply provide an answer to a question. These more advanced exams share with first language exam essays the requirement that opinions are supported by reference to the student's knowledge of the world and their experience.

If students do not do well in terms of all the skills tested in a particular exam, clearly they will lose marks. It is not possible to compensate for a deficiency in one area by excelling in another. For example, no matter how faultless students' grammar might be, if they have covered only some of the required points, they will only be given some of the marks. Similarly, they may also be penalized for using the wrong register or layout, and this in turn will inevitably prevent their writing having the desired effect on the target reader. If they produce a faultless answer in the form of a letter, when what was required was a brochure, then again they will lose marks.

Assessing written work and providing feedback

If students are to benefit fully from the time and effort we put into marking their written work, it is important that we and they do as much with it as possible. There should be a process in which work is revised several times and analysed before being filed for future reference. It can be very heartening for students to look back at what they did in the early stages of the course and see how much progress they have made, so we should make sure our students do this from time to time as they move through the course. Their written work files can form the basis of a personal error checklist which they can then use in the exam.

What criteria should be used to assess written work?

The criteria used to assess written work should be as close as possible to those used in the exam itself. While some exam boards readily provide handbooks with details of scales used in assessment, graded sample answers, and examiners' comments, others play their cards closer to their chests. Even so, it is generally stated somewhere in the material about the exam that form, content, and task achievement are all regarded as important.

We should assess students' work in the lead-up to the exam in terms of the same criteria. To make sure that we are doing this, it is useful to give a mark out of five or ten for each aspect of the writing process that is being assessed, e.g. task achievement (the inclusion of all the points in the rubric, producing a text of the right length), range and appropriacy of vocabulary used, layout conventions, appropriate register, formal accuracy, and so on. Marks for each criterion can be added up to give an overall grade.

Assessing written work is a responsibility that can be shared with students. The teacher can make up a checklist based on the criteria used in the exam they are taking, if available, or use the one below.

Have you checked your work carefully for mistakes with the following:
* spelling?
* basic grammar?
* punctuation?

Have you followed the instructions for:
* length?
* the kind of text you are supposed to write?
* points to include?

How do you think someone reading your letter, article, brochure, report etc. would react?
A Very well
B Quite well
C OK
D Not very well
E Badly

The last question on that checklist could be used as the basis for a grade, though in the early stages of the course the teacher may not wish to give numerical or letter grades at all. Later in the course we will need to give marks, but these should be in keeping with the stage we have reached in the course. We should only grade strictly in accordance with the level expected in the exam in the final weeks of the course.

Although to some teachers it may seem an extreme approach, asking students to grade their own work helps them to think critically and is, therefore, a very useful practice, especially in the weeks immediately before the exam (by which time they should have a good appreciation of the relevant criteria).

Providing feedback

Students are generally very interested in a numerical or letter grade, but it is important that they understand exactly where their strengths and weaknesses lie. We should therefore always try to write at least a brief comment on their work where we mention task achievement – responding to the piece of writing as the target reader might do – before we go on to indicate what mark we give the piece or to comment on errors of form, accuracy, and so on. It is also very motivating for students if we comment positively on some aspect of their work. If they can see there is something to build on, they are more likely to take the trouble to revise their work and to try harder in future. Here is an example of the kind of comment we might write:

> You make some very interesting points about the problems with the canteen. It certainly sounds as if there are a lot of things that need to be changed. I was really pleased to see that you tried to use some of the linking expressions we studied in Unit 5. Well done! This would be a better report if you had used headings (see p.12 of the 'Writing Reference'). I've marked some other things you need to correct. Please revise your work and give it back to me next week.

Either we, or our students, should keep a record of our comments and other corrections so that when revised versions are handed in, we can see that the learners have made an attempt to deal with any problems. One very manageable way of doing this is getting students to send in their work by email. If we establish a separate file for each student, we can then see at a glance how well they have coped with the revision process. We can also build up a bank of typical errors and problems, which we can use as a basis for class work. Extracts from students' work can be pasted into worksheets or projected onto a screen and these can be analysed and discussed in class.

Dealing with errors of form

Exam boards are only really hard on errors that impede communication or which are seen as being below the level expected in that particular exam. When we mark written work it is best to concentrate on those errors which will be significant in the exam. It is discouraging for students to get written work back covered in corrections and changes, particularly if these are errors they could not possibly be expected to be able to correct themselves.

It is a good idea to use a correction code rather than simply writing in the correct form. This will mean that students gradually develop the ability to edit their own work rather than relying on the teacher. The development of this ability is particularly valuable in exam writing courses. We could use a ready-made correction code, such as is provided in Chapter 7 of Harmer's companion volume in this series, *How to Teach Writing*, or create one in collaboration with our students using extracts from their work. This is particularly helpful, as it allows students to see worked examples of the most typical errors for people at their level.

How to help students to deal with task input
The most important thing in relation to preparing students for writing tests is that the more opportunity they have to write, the better prepared they will be. There is no substitute for writing practice; this should lead to feedback, but it is important to consider the possibility that some of this feedback can come from other students. If students give one another feedback, it encourages constructive interaction between class members, will help them to think more critically about their own work, and will considerably ease the burden on the teacher, in terms of marking.

Because writing is essentially a time-consuming and (usually) individual activity, teachers are sometimes uneasy about timetabling enough written practice. This is in some ways sensible, since spending half or more of a fifty-minute lesson with everyone working individually in silence may indeed be making less than optimal use of time that could be spent with the class interacting with one another or with the teacher. The solution is to assign most of the actual writing as homework. Class time will then be spent on the following areas, each of which allows for student–student, teacher–student, or teacher–whole-class interaction.

Reading and analysing task rubrics

Given that exam tasks can be very complex, it is essential that students get plenty of practice in identifying task demands when reading rubrics, particularly when there is also input of some kind to deal with. The practice activities described here can be done in an extended lesson, or the individual activities can be done at different times:

Example lesson

The teacher gives out worksheets with several authentic exam tasks accompanied by true/false questions, as in the examples on page 52. In the first example, key words have already been underlined and the true/false questions answered. Students work individually answering the true/false

Read these exam tasks (1–3) and underline the key words. Then decide if the statements that follow the tasks are true or false. The first one has been done for you as an example.

1   You have been doing a class project on <u>young people and work</u>. <u>Your teacher</u> has asked you to write an <u>essay</u> giving <u>your opinion</u> on the following statement:

<u>It is a good thing</u> for <u>students</u> to have <u>part-time</u> jobs while they are studying.

Write your **essay** using between 120 and 180 words.

a   You are supposed to write a report on the project. *False*
b   You are supposed to say what you think about young people and work. *True*
c   You can disagree with the statement if you want to. *True*
d   You can use a lot of informal expressions if you want to. *False*

2   You see this advertisement in a local English language newspaper:

PRACTISE YOUR ENGLISH

We are looking for students of English to spend one morning a week working with elderly English speakers living locally. Good pay and conditions for the right people and a chance to win a trip to England for two, all expenses paid. Write to Dr Ronald Murdoch, Happy Days Estate, PO Box 219 with information about your level of English, your experience with the elderly, and your availability.

You have decided to apply for one of these jobs.

Write your **application** using between 120 and 180 words.

a   You are supposed to write a formal letter.
b   In your letter you can say how good your English is, when you are available, and how much experience you have had, but you don't have to.
c   You should not mention pay and conditions or the trip to England.
d   You should start your letter by saying where you saw the advertisement and telling the reader that you are a student.

3   You see this advertisement in a local English language newspaper:

Under 25 magazine is looking for articles in answer to the question, 'Is life better for today's young people than it was for their parents?' There will be a prize of a trip for two to Disneyland Paris for the best article we receive.

Write your **article** using between 120 and 180 words.

a   You can write a letter asking about the trip to Disneyland Paris in answer to this question.
b   You should use very formal language in your answer.
c   You are supposed to discuss the question starting, 'Is life better … ?'.
d   You will get paid for your article in euros.

questions and underlining key words in the task rubrics to justify their answers before comparing with a partner. Answers are then checked with the whole class, eliciting the key words that should be underlined.

The teacher gives out another worksheet with task rubrics and asks students to work in groups underlining key words, i.e. words that indicate the task requirements. Each group gives feedback as the answers are checked in open class. The students then choose one of the tasks to answer for homework.

The teacher gives out copies of the following:

1 An authentic exam task

2 A 'sample' answer that does not satisfy some or all of the task demands (These are sometimes available in exam handbooks.)

Students work individually, locating parts of the rubric and task input that are not answered in the sample text. They should then compare their work with a partner before checking in open class. Finally, they can be asked to write an 'improved' version of the sample answer, either in class or for homework.

Dealing with the elements of task input

As we have seen, many exams include extensive task input (i.e. the rubric itself and textual and visual material, including notes, graphs, and diagrams). This represents several challenges to students. Firstly, many students simply do not read the input carefully enough. They need to be reminded frequently to do this, and to understand that they will be penalized if they do not include all the points demanded by the task. They also need to learn to integrate points from the input into their own writing in an appropriate fashion. Candidates who lift elements from the input wholesale lose marks, so students need to be trained to paraphrase rather than copy. Finally, they are often expected to add some of their own ideas and to integrate these with the points from the input. This is not always stated in the rubric and students may be unaware that it is expected of them. Here is an approach to dealing with the task input issue.

Example lesson

Give out a worksheet with an authentic exam task. Learners look at the task and assess a model text in terms of how far it meets the task demands and/or they answer open-ended or true/false questions about the task (teachers can write the model text themselves, or find a published example of such an activity in a coursebook).

Students work individually on the questions before comparing answers with a partner and then checking in open class. They then work with the same partner on planning their answers. Guidance can be given, especially in the early stages of the course. The completed plans can be written up on OHP sheets and discussed in the next class. Work can be done on paraphrasing individual elements relating to the input but the rest of the writing can be done at home, to be revised in pairs in a subsequent class.

Each student can be given a checklist to make sure all the elements from the input have been integrated.

Where input is in the form of graphs, tables, or statistics students may need help in dealing with these; an awareness-raising approach where they match elements of this kind of input to sample answers works well.

Encouraging familiarity with genres

Students may not have had experience of producing some of the genres tested, even in their first language. Unsurprisingly, they may find it difficult to produce them in English. There are various ways we can deal with this lack of familiarity:

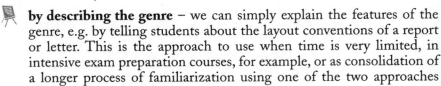

by describing the genre – we can simply explain the features of the genre, e.g. by telling students about the layout conventions of a report or letter. This is the approach to use when time is very limited, in intensive exam preparation courses, for example, or as consolidation of a longer process of familiarization using one of the two approaches below.

by providing annotated models – the second approach is to provide models of key genres accompanied by annotations. Many coursebooks use this approach. Activities within coursebook units on various genres students need to produce in the exam are often cross-referenced to annotated examples in a writing guide appendix. An example is given on page 55 (top). Some bilingual dictionaries also include models of key genres which can be used for analysis and commentary.

by getting students to analyse the genre – the third approach involves getting students to analyse authentic or semi-authentic examples of the genre and identify the key features themselves. This is obviously the most time-consuming of the three approaches, but it can be extremely rewarding for both teacher and students. We can either gather examples of the genres ourselves or set up a genre collection task where students find their own texts. Online newspapers provide excellent sources of articles, reviews, and even letters. Students preparing for university entrance English tests like IELTS or TOEFL should be able to provide examples of essays, and business English students might have access to memos, letters, reports, and proposals in English. By writing to businesses, tourist information offices, schools, and colleges, it should also be possible to make a collection of brochures, leaflets, information sheets, instructions, and directions. This approach also provides valuable practice with letter writing and an absolutely authentic means of checking that the letter has produced the desired response in the reader.

If this seems too ambitious a project for our students, we could use reading texts as a basis for genre analysis. Ideally, this material will include examples of all the genres students are expected to produce. It should be borne in mind that most coursebook reading texts are adapted newspaper, magazine, or journal articles and therefore provide examples of only one or two genres. Published materials do,

How should I structure a formal letter?

Begin a formal letter in one of these ways:

- *Dear Mr/Mrs/Miss/Ms Lodge* – use the person's title and surname if you know it.
- *Dear Sir/Madam* if you don't know the person's name or whether they are a man or a woman. ——————

Say why you are writing. Clearly state the subject or context. ——————

Organise all the essential information from the task prompts in a clear and logical way in the main paragraphs of the letter. You may need to add some extra ideas of your own.

Say how you expect the other person to respond to your letter if this is appropriate. ——————

Finish your letter in one of these ways:

Yours sincerely, if you have started your letter with the name of the person you are writing to.

Yours faithfully, if you have started your letter *Dear Sir/Madam.* ——————

Dear Sir/Madam,

I am writing to complain about the prize I was sent for winning your 'Travel and Learn' competition for language learners. There are four different problems with the pack I received.

Firstly, the language pack you sent was for learners of Russian, not English. I clearly remember ticking the 'English' box. In addition to this, the textbook mentioned in the advert was missing and one of the two audio cassettes was broken and impossible to play.

Furthermore, I watched the Russian video and I am afraid to say that the picture quality was very poor. I hope this is not typical of your videos.

Naturally, I am still interested in learning English, and I would be grateful if you could send me the correct pack. However, I am not prepared to return the Russian pack until I have received the replacement and checked the contents carefully. I also expect to receive a full refund for the cost of returning the Russian pack to you.

I look forward to hearing from you.

Yours faithfully,

(Name)

From *First Certificate Masterclass Student's Book*
by Simon Haines & Barbara Stewart (Oxford University Press)

---

nevertheless, include other genres in listening activities, grammar and vocabulary tasks, or as input for speaking work. By making use of this material, we should be able to offer our students a full range of genres for analysis. Once we have a reasonable collection of texts, we can set tasks in which students examine the following areas (page 56).

Learners should be able to arrive at a list of prototypical features or 'dos and don'ts' similar to the annotations in the example above. They will also have found functional expressions and vocabulary that occur frequently in these genres.

Coursebook writing guides, and bilingual and learners' dictionaries also often list key vocabulary and functional language for the various genres, as in the example on page 57.

formal and informal style features	salutations (*Dear Dr Bell*, *Hi Mary* etc), contractions, vocabulary, grammatical structures
layout features	presence/absence of headings, bullet points, paragraphing etc.
staging	typical openings and closings, obligatory and optional elements, e.g. stating the reason for writing at the outset of a formal letter; apologizing for silence at the beginning of an informal letter
structures and vocabulary that occur in a number of examples	typical ways of dealing with staging, e.g. *I am writing + to + enquire about .../ apply for.../ complain about .../ express my thanks/disgust/appreciation* etc.

How to prepare students for writing exam answers

Helping students to generate ideas and to plan their writing

Students may not have had much experience of drawing on their own opinions and ideas to write exam answers. They will therefore need support and practice with generating ideas. The most common and effective method for doing this is **brainstorming**, i.e. generating as many ideas as possible, some of which will later be rejected or modified.

If brainstorming is completely unfamiliar, we can begin by showing students a list of 'brainstormed' points for potential inclusion in a piece of writing (this can be a list of points generated by the teacher or something from a published source). The point is to make it clear that pretty much anything that comes into one's head can be noted down. Then we can try the brainstorming technique as an open-class activity in which everyone is encouraged to chip in with an idea or two. In larger classes, it is a good idea to divide the class into smaller groups and give each group a limited time to come up with five ideas for possible inclusion. The groups then report back and the ideas are written up on the board.

In the case of brainstorming opinions 'for' and 'against', if students have no particularly strong views on a subject, brainstorming may prove more successful if they try to list the opinions of someone they know well (an older relative, or a boyfriend, or a girlfriend) or even a famous person.

Many students also need help with **planning**. They may not be convinced of its importance nor fully understand the relationship between planning and the final product. A model text is one possible starting point in one approach to making this relationship clearer for students. Students read the text and compare it to a plan, marking sections of the text that correspond to each part of the plan. At a later stage they can be asked to decide which of two plans produced the model text. The plans themselves can be used as the basis for the overall structure of a range of texts of the same type (discursive, narrative, review, instructions).

It is also important for students to see how plans are connected to the task rubric. For example, they can be given an exam task and two or three alternative plans, and asked to decide which of the plans would produce the most successful answer to the task, as in the example shown on page 58.

Dear Louise,

My friend, Emily, has started to watch far too much television. In fact, that's all she does. She never wants to come out anymore and the only time she goes outside her home is to go to school. She watches anything that comes on, but mainly movies, some of which are very violent or contain an excessive amount of bad language. This is beginning to affect her behavior, as she is now using bad language herself and acting aggressively towards other people. What can I do to help her to realize that this is not good for her and that she shouldn't spend so much time glued to the television? Please help!

Letter:
Louise has asked readers to write giving suggestions on how to deal with this problem. Louise will publish some of the letters. Write a letter which begins, 'Dear Reader, …'

Dear Reader,

I am eighteen years old, and I decided to write this letter because I faced a similar problem with my best friend, so I think I can offer some helpful advice.

First, you have to talk to your friend and find out if she has any other problems. Is she shy? Does she have low self-esteem and feels she should shut herself away? Is she facing family problems? Is she watching violent movies because her own life is boring? It seems to me that watching too much TV and shutting herself away from her friends is just an attempt to escape from her real problem. If you talk to her caringly, you can make her trust you, and then she will confess the real reasons why she is doing this.

If this approach doesn't work, perhaps you should try and get her to see a counselor. An expert has the experience to help your friend deal with her feelings and overcome her problem. By explaining the consequences of cutting herself off from other people and living in a 'fantasy' world, a counselor can help her see how she is missing out on life. A counselor can also suggest some solutions, like taking up a hobby, or making up with her family if this is the real cause of her problems.

I think it is worth trying to help somebody, so keep on trying and don't forget that there is always a solution to a problem.

Yours,

1 Topic vocabulary
glued to the television
excessive bad language
violent movies
watch/see a movie
My favorite types of movies are …
low self-esteem
escape from reality

2 Useful vocabulary – Giving advice
Why don't you …?
My advice (to you) is …
Have you considered …?
If I were you …
How about …?
I suggest …
One solution might be to …
Another answer would be to …

From *Michigan ECCE Gold Exam Maximiser*
by Jain Cook (Longman)

You may be asked in an examination for a description of an ideal house, parent, pet, or something similar. In many ways this is a straightforward composition. However, its disadvantages are that it is more difficult for you to demonstrate the full range of your writing abilities.

Which of the three approaches below would be the most suitable for answering this question?

Describe the ideal pet for a young child.

OUTLINE 1 general introduction about pets – description of your childhood pet – its looks, personality, etc.; adventures you used to have – when you got it, how long you had it, who looked after it – problems and difficulties you used to have – what happened to the pet in the end

OUTLINE 2 take a number of examples and discuss advantages and disadvantages – dogs, cats, hamsters, rabbits; discuss problems of keeping dogs in cities – mess on pavements, etc.; problems of what to do if the animal gets lost; cost of keeping an animal; conclude by pointing out that many people don't like animals

OUTLINE 3 general introduction; purpose of giving a pet to a child – emotional and educational – characteristics of an animal that would make a good pet, ie good nature, practical considerations, such as where child lives, parents, etc.; conclude with short list of choices

From *Proficiency Masterclass Student's Book, First Edition* by Cathy Gude & Michael Duckworth (Oxford University Press)

Students also need to understand the relationship between brainstormed points and planning. They can begin by deciding which points should be eliminated and are then asked to organize the remaining points into sections of the plan. There are many published activities of this type.

Finally, teachers need to demonstrate the transitions from points in a plan to connected text. Once again, we can start with the text and work backwards to the plan, asking students to underline words and expressions used to link points. They can then be given practice with the linkers as in the example on page 59.

Training students to revise their own work

Before students submit work they should be given an opportunity to revise it. Initially, this works best as a pair-work activity, either in class or via email. Students of similar achievement levels should be paired and asked to exchange and comment on each other's work. We can actually make this paired revision process part of the task by getting learners to annotate their work, explaining the revisions their partner suggested and any dictionary or grammar reference research they have done to resolve doubts.

This kind of approach works particularly well if we have previously established a means of working in class in which student writing is revised collaboratively. Here is one approach:

Students copy their work onto overhead slides and also make sufficient paper copies to distribute to everyone in the class. Each piece of work is displayed on the projector and copies distributed. The teacher invites comments from the student who wrote the piece; these should include things the student feels pleased with and things they are uncertain about. The teacher then elicits, from the rest of the class

1 Look at these points a student has written down to include in a composition about task 1 from Exercise 1. Decide if the points support the statement or offer the opposite point of view. Mark them ☺ or ☹.

> 1 It is a good idea for young people to take some time off to travel before they start work or university.

Travelling is fun and you can have lots of adventures. ☐

It can be difficult to settle down when you come back. ☐

You can get to know other cultures. ☐

You can make friends with people from all over the world. ☐

You can feel homesick. ☐

Travelling can be exhausting and even dangerous. ☐

2 Combine the points into two paragraphs using the linking words below.

There are several obvious benefits of taking some time off to travel. Firstly and perhaps most obviously,
(1) .... In addition, (2) ....
and this may help you in later life. Another benefit is that (3) ....
and even learn their languages.
Nevertheless, some young travellers experience difficulties. Unfortunately,
(4) ....
particularly if you travel alone.
Furthermore, if you don't have travelling companions, (5) ....
A third disadvantage is that
(6) .... and this may affect your studies or your work.

Adapted from *New First Certificate Gold Exam Maximiser* by Sally Burgess, with Jacky Newbrook & Judith Wilson (Longman)

further comments; these should include questions about the meaning or appropriateness of words and expressions, suggested revisions and corrections. Everybody makes any agreed changes and corrections on their copy of the piece and keeps this in a written work dossier.

By using this method, we can do much of our 'marking' in class with the students present. This has obvious advantages, not least that we can ensure both that we have understood what the student was trying to say and that they have understood any corrections or changes.

Over time, students become comfortable about commenting on their classmates' work and can work very effectively with a partner. They either make the suggested corrections on the spot or use a correction code. The use of such a code introduces a further revision stage and generally ensures that when work finally reaches the teacher, there is much less to correct.

We can then use the code and comment on the piece before returning it to the student for further revision. They should try to make the necessary changes and revisions, either on their own or with a partner, and then resubmit their work. Before returning it to them to be filed, we can write in any correct forms that the student has been unable to find her- or himself.

Giving students timed writing practice

As the exam approaches, it is important to give students the experience of writing to a time limit. So as to avoid a situation where students panic and forget all the work they have done on analysing task input, brainstorming, planning, writing, and revising their work, it is a good idea to introduce timed practice in these stages. The teacher can begin by giving students an exam task and setting a five-minute time limit for analysis of the input. Then a second time limit is set for brainstorming, a third for planning, a fourth for writing, and a final limit for revising what has been written. Gradually, we build up to an exam-authentic situation where students are given a task and write their answers within a strictly monitored period of time.

Debunking misconceptions

Rumours about ways of getting better marks in all the exams discussed in this book circulate freely by word of mouth and on the Internet. Some of these offer sound advice, but it is a good idea to make sure that our students are not operating under any false assumptions. The following are three of the most common misconceptions.

- **'Memorizing perfect answers is a good idea'** – a surprising number of students believe that it is possible – or even advisable – to memorize a perfect answer and then regurgitate it in the exam itself. The chances of this strategy succeeding are almost nil and students should be told this in no uncertain terms.

  To begin with, most exam boards prepare new papers for each exam session. They do not recycle questions in exactly the same form and it is highly unlikely that a memorized answer will incorporate the same input, fulfil task requirements, or have the desired effect on the imagined reader. Memorizing a text of the required length so well that one can reproduce it word for word probably takes more time and effort than learning to write well in the first place. Even in TOEFL, where the titles are published beforehand, it would be impossible to memorize answers to several hundred questions and there is no guarantee that the one or two one does happen to memorize will actually come up. It is usually easy to detect memorized text because it is seldom memorized perfectly. If examiners believe an answer has been memorized, it is marked down.

- **'Answers a few words over or under the limit fail'** – there are also some common fallacies with regard to length requirements. Many students believe that the examiners actually count the number of words and that if they have written a few words over or under the limit, their answer will not be marked. This is not true, though they should, of course, aim to reach – but not go too far over – the limit. An answer more than 10% above or below the limits will usually be penalized, though it will still be read and assessed.

  Another assumption about length is that it is better to write more. Teachers should point out that if students write a lot more than they are asked for, they will be marked down for task achievement, as they have essentially changed the task. There is a lot of difference between writing a 180-word letter and a 300-word letter. (See Task File: Task B to experience what it is like to write to such a strict word limit.)

- **'It is better to spend your time writing one really good answer than two mediocre ones'** – a common misconception is the idea that, in exams where more than one answer is required, it is better to answer one question very well than the required number of questions moderately well. Again, this strategy would normally result in disaster. Although the second of the two questions in IELTS is given more weight, it must be emphasized to students that they are very unlikely to produce a faultless answer that gains the highest possible grade. Even a poor answer to the first question would win them some marks. If they don't even attempt an answer, they are effectively throwing away a large proportion of the available marks.

Teaching students to make good use of their time in the exam

In some exams there is plenty of time; in others there is considerable pressure. Whenever there are time constraints, in exams where students must answer more than one question, they should divide the total time according to the relative mark weighting of the questions (unless specified otherwise on the paper, this is usually an even division). The time spent on each answer should then be divided among the following steps:

1 Reading the rubric and task input (if any) and circling or underlining key words
2 Brainstorming ideas
3 Planning
4 Writing
5 Revising

Writing will take up the largest proportion of the time and roughly equal amounts should usually be devoted to the other steps. Students should always aim to leave enough time to read their work through and revise it. It is useful to encourage them to do this systematically. They can even create their own checklist of typical errors, memorize it, and then look for these mistakes in the exam itself. They should, however, be discouraged from attempting to write a piece out again. This is unnecessary, as long as they have made any corrections and changes clearly and neatly. The need for major rewriting is usually the result of inefficient – or non-existent – planning.

In exams where there is a lot of time pressure, the planning stage may have to be very short and might involve noting down a few expressions or points for inclusion. In both IELTS and TOEFL, students can be taught a basic schema that can be applied to a range of titles. If they are sufficiently familiar with this, they should be able to activate it in the exam without having to write it down.

Handwriting and presentation

Nowadays, many of us are relatively unaccustomed to writing more than a few words without a screen and keyboard, particularly under time pressure. Some of our students may experience additional difficulty if they come from languages that use a different script, but even those who share our alphabet may be more comfortable with a keyboard than a pen. University students, although generally used to taking notes, may still find it hard to write neatly and legibly in an exam setting. Examiners are, of course, tolerant of variation in handwriting, but if we have students whose handwriting is very difficult to read, we will need to point this out to them at the beginning of the course, and perhaps help them to find resources (e.g. books or websites) for improving handwriting.

All students should be encouraged to test out different pens. Changing the kind of pen used can improve legibility, writing speed, comfort, and neatness considerably. Candidates should normally write their answers in ink. Pencil is unacceptable to some exam boards and creates an impression of tentativeness and impermanence that may have a negative effect on the reader.

Exam answers are expected to be neat and legible but they need not be completely devoid of any evidence of revision and correction. Students should not waste valuable time with correction fluid and the like in the exam itself. They should, of course, cross out anything they wish the examiner to disregard. This also applies to any brainstorming notes, plans, or rough drafts. In some cases, these are written on separate sheets of paper specifically for rough work. For security reasons (i.e. so that details of questions cannot be passed on to people in other centres where the same paper will be taken later), rough work is often collected at the end of the exam session and then destroyed. Students need not worry that the examiner will see their rough work.

It is important for candidates to indicate clearly where their answer to a question begins and ends. There is no need to write out the questions but, if there are several options, students should indicate which question(s) they have chosen to answer. If their answer goes on to a second or third page, they should number the pages. In this way, they can be sure that they will be assessed on the basis of what they really intend to present to the examiner, namely the carefully planned and meticulously revised piece of writing they have worked so hard to produce.

Conclusions

In this chapter we have:
- listed the characteristics common to many writing tests.
- looked at the task types used in these tests.
- listed the various abilities measured in writing tests.
- emphasized the importance of task achievement among the abilities measured.
- suggested appropriate ways of responding to students' writing.
- argued that students should be encouraged to participate in the assessment of written work.
- listed stages in the writing process that can be addressed interactively in class.
- provided an approach for helping students deal with task rubrics.
- suggested methods of familiarizing students with tested genres.
- explained the role of brainstorming and planning, and provided approaches to presenting these to students.
- outlined a method of revising student writing in class.
- discussed possible misconceptions students may have about writing exams.

- identified the stages in the exam writing process and suggested how much time should be allotted to each in the exam itself.
- considered the issues of handwriting and presentation.

5 How to teach grammar and vocabulary for exams

- General approaches to teaching grammar and vocabulary for exams
- Common exam tasks
- Criteria used to assess grammar and vocabulary
- Helping learners get to grips with grammar and vocabulary

General approaches to teaching grammar and vocabulary for exams

By the time learners begin seriously to prepare for an exam, there should be no significant areas of grammar and vocabulary, relative to the level of the exam, that they have not already been taught. A period of exam preparation is not the time to start presenting large amounts of new language; rather, it is a time for reviewing and consolidating what has already been learned, with a view to achieving complete mastery of it.

Practice tasks should therefore be designed to encourage learners to use the knowledge they already have, with confidence, and to notice where there are gaps in that knowledge. Learners should also be encouraged to explore and expand the range of grammar and vocabulary that they can put into active use. Practice tasks should motivate learners to find things out for themselves. They should highlight study techniques which develop independent learning, and provide guidance on the use of reference materials such as grammar books and dictionaries.

An important principle underlying the incorporation of grammar and vocabulary into the syllabus is that they should be studied in context. Extracts of written text and transcriptions of listening material can be used to draw the learners' attention to the way in which a particular word or grammatical item has been used, and why. The reasons why particular forms of language are appropriate or correct should be explicitly discussed. This approach helps learners to develop awareness of stylistic differences between similar words and expressions, as well as requiring them to notice the features of the surrounding context that determine the choice and form of a particular word or phrase.

Since exam success depends on using language accurately and appropriately, error correction activities can be used to develop learners' attention to detail, and sensitivity to incorrect and inappropriate uses of language. Finally, as the course progresses, practice tasks should reflect more closely the sorts of tasks that test grammar and vocabulary in the exam itself.

common exam tasks

In many English language exams, the candidate's knowledge and use of grammar and vocabulary is tested in tasks which are skills-focused (reading, writing, speaking, or listening). However, there are some exams which include tasks designed to focus explicitly on the candidate's control of language structure, grammar, and vocabulary. Some of the more common task types are described here.

Gap-fill tasks

A **multiple choice** gap-fill task offers the candidate a choice of possible answers to fill each of the gaps in a sentence or text. The right answer must not only make sense but must also fit grammatically, so awareness of sentence structure is vital. Learners need to be trained to examine the gapped sentence and to predict the sort of answer that is needed to complete the sentence, before they look at the three or four choices offered. Only one of the choices will fit the sentence correctly, and it is easier to make the right choice if you already have an idea of what you are looking for. Here are two examples – a Michigan ECCE example at CEF level B2 (ALTE level 3) testing a grammatical structure, and a Michigan ECPE example at CEF level C2 (ALTE level 5) testing a vocabulary item:

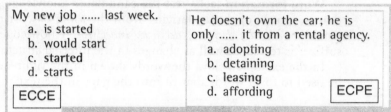

My new job ...... last week.
- a. is started
- b. would start
- **c. started**
- d. starts

ECCE

He doesn't own the car; he is only ...... it from a rental agency.
- a. adopting
- b. detaining
- **c. leasing**
- d. affording

ECPE

From *Michigan Certificate Examinations Information Bulletin 2002–2003*

More complex gap-fill tasks involve inserting whole phrases, rather than single words, into a gap. This is particularly demanding when dealing with isolated sentences, since making the correct choice depends on recognizing the structural features in the sentence:

11. _____ mixed with a base such as egg yolk was the exclusive medium for painting panels in the Middle Ages.
- (A) Finely ground pigments
- (B) It is a finely ground pigment
- (C) A finely ground pigment
- (D) That a finely ground pigment

From *Cambridge Preparation for the TOEFL Test*
by Jolene Gear & Robert Gear (Cambridge University Press)

In order to choose the correct answer (C), the student must notice that the verb *was* is in the singular form (so the answer can't be A), that there is no relative clause in the sentence (so B is impossible), and that *mixed* is not a finite use of the verb (which might have been a reason to choose D).

A **cloze test** is a kind of gap-fill task. It uses a text from which words have been deleted at more or less regular intervals. The task is to think of a suitable word to fill each of the gaps. While in many gap-fill tasks the candidate is given a set of possible answers, in a cloze test they must find their own word, using the context to determine the kind of word which will fit grammatically and with the right meaning, as shown here:

> The reality is that **(0)** ....*everyone*.... uses jargon. It is an essential part of the network of occupations and pursuits **(1)** .... make up society. All jobs have an element of jargon, which workers learn **(2)** .... they develop their expertise. All hobbies require mastery of a jargon. Each society grouping has **(3)** .... jargon. The phenomenon **(4)** .... out to be universal – and valuable.
>
> From *Objective CAE – Student Book* by Felicity O'Dell & Annie Broadhead (Cambridge University Press)

Occasionally, a gap will allow more than one correct answer; if so, this is allowed for in the marking scheme.

Word formation tasks test the candidate's knowledge of word families, that is, groups of words deriving from the same base or root. An example would be *decide, decision, decisive, indecisive*. Knowledge of prefixes and suffixes is tested, as well as changes in the internal structure of words.

In the example below, the words shown in the right-hand column must be used to form words that fit into the gaps in the text:

> **WHY DO PEOPLE TAKE RISKS?**
>
> Why are some people risk-takers? What makes them take part in **(0)** .*dangerous*.. or even life-threatening activities? There are different **(1)** .... for this. Car racers love the **(2)** .... of speed, while climbers get their thrills from **(3)** .... the challenge of high mountains. Millions of years ago, when people faced danger daily, risk-taking was essential for **(4)** .... Although living in today's world is **(5)** .... than it was in those days, perhaps that **(6)** .... instinct still remains. However, taking risks can become a very **(7)** .... obsession. Some people can even become addicted to danger, and are unable to stop looking for it. It is also **(8)** .... that the majority of risk-takers seem to be men. Is this because men have more **(9)** .... ? Or do women think twice about taking risks because they are more **(10)** .... ?
>
> | 0 | DANGER |
> | 1 | EXPLAIN |
> | 2 | EXCITE |
> | 3 | FACE |
> | 4 | SURVIVE |
> | 5 | EASE |
> | 6 | BASE |
> | 7 | HEALTH |
> | 8 | INTEREST |
> | 9 | CURIOUS |
> | 10 | SENSE |
>
> Adapted from *New First Certificate Gold* by Newbrook, Wilson & Acklam (Longman)

Students can prepare for this sort of task by developing their awareness of common patterns of word variation. They can look for the different forms of words in dictionaries (sometimes they are grouped together) and write them on a grid, as shown below. It may be possible to post such a grid on the classroom wall, and add examples to it as the class encounters them.

Noun	Verb	Adjective	Adverb
decision	decide	(in)decisive	(in)decisively
success	succeed	(un)successful	(un)successfully

Text-matching exercises

The ability to make sense of the relationships between ideas in a text, using structural and vocabulary clues, is tested in exercises which involve organizing sections of a text into the right order. Candidates may be asked to sort sentences or paragraphs into sequence, or to fill gaps with other sections of text. For practice purposes, it can be helpful to photocopy exercises such as the one below and cut the list of phrases into strips so that they can be physically moved around and arranged in order. Handling them encourages learners to study their features more closely and focus on clues that indicate how they fit grammatically into the longer text. To make the exercise more difficult, there are more phrases than gaps.

TRAVEL HOTELS

Room for revolution

Electronic gadgets have moved out of the office and into the hotel bedroom in a big way. Gone are the days when smart city-centre hotels provided mere B & B with a few in-room luxuries thrown in.

5   Today's travellers are less interested in clothes hangers and hairdryers than in-room fax machines and natty TV sets that let them pay the bill, (0) _J_ . Some people even predict that tomorrow's globetrotters won't waste any time in the lobby when they roll up at
10 their hotel for the night. They'll check themselves in on an in-room monitor, heat up a snack in their wall-mounted microwave and then (1)____. While personal service will remain a premium at the top end of the market, technology will (2)____.
15   Hotels geared to push-button living now provide personal pagers, extra phone lines for fax and computers, in-room answering machines, magnetic door keys and touch-screens which can (3)____. Bedside remote controls enable guests to flick through a score of TV
20 channels, turn up the temperature and (4)____. Should

push-button living make guests lazy, hotels are also jacking up the high-tech content of their gyms. Videos to plug into while pumping iron are now commonplace, while staff will often (5)____.
25   Whether microchips will ultimately replace the personal touch at tomorrow's leading hotels remains to be seen. Robots are unlikely to (6)____. However, there's little doubt that properties with up-to-the-second communications technology will steal a march on the
30 competition.
  Will tomorrow's travellers gladly swap 21st century gadgets for a helping of good old-fashioned service? The chances are they will have checked out on their TV screen and be halfway to the plane before anyone thinks to ask.

A	draw the curtains without stirring from under the duvet
B	hit the exit command on their display screen
C	include training programmes in its charges
D	decide where most of the business goes
E	start steaming suits and pouring coffee
F	deliver exercise bikes to the room on request
G	show everything from messages to weather reports
H	press a few buttons to check out next day
I	offer tangible benefits to guests rather than staff
J	check share prices and watch movies

From *Advanced Masterclass CAE – Student Book*
by Tricia Aspinall & Annette Capel (Oxford University Press)

Sentence transformation tasks

This type of task introduces a 'key' word that is to be used, in the given form to transform the sentence into a new grammatical form without changing its meaning. Here is an example:

> Could I possibly borrow your mobile phone?
> **mind**
> Would you .... me your mobile phone?

Learners need plenty of practice to familiarize themselves with the sentence patterns and changes that are likely to appear in these tasks. Common types of transformation include direct speech to reported speech, comparison (e.g. from *Jane is a far better swimmer than her sister* to *Jane's sister doesn't swim nearly as well as she does*), constructions with modal verbs (such as the example above), from a sentence using the past simple tense to one using the present perfect. There are between six and ten sentence transformations in a typical exam paper.

Error identification and correction tasks

Some exam tasks focus on identifying incorrect uses of English. The task may be made more difficult in that four possible mistakes are highlighted, of which only one is actually wrong, as in these TOEIC examples:

> **150.** Instability in the government has led to a lower
>   A   B   C
> in the growth rate of the economy.
>   D
>
> **159.** Because the workers accept a pay cut, they may
>   A   B
> find themselves without jobs.
>   C   D
>
> From *Oxford Preparation Course for the TOEIC Test – Student Book* (Oxford University Press)

Alternatively, students may have to check each line of a text, to find and correct the mistake in it. There may be some lines with no mistake, as here:

> I dont know about you but my favourite day of the week   **don't**
> is friday. You have all the pleasure of being able to   **Friday**
> look forward to the weekend and its the day when you   **it's**
> can go out without worrying about homework.   ✓

Students preparing for an exam will be doing a lot of written work, so it is important to train them to check their own work for mistakes in spelling, punctuation, and grammar. They should learn to expect the teacher not to correct work, but rather to mark it with an indication of the number and type of errors made. The more they are encouraged to pay attention to their own language mistakes, the easier they will find this type of exam task.

Accuracy and appropriacy

By the time they reach CEF level B2 (ALTE level 3), learners are expected to show confidence in their handling of the main structures of English. This confidence derives from knowing which are the right words to use and how they fit together into sentences. Language which is not sufficiently accurate or appropriate can impede communication, and may well create the wrong effect on the reader or listener.

Knowledge of collocations

Words and phrases which appear to be very similar in meaning are often distinguished from each other by the different ways in which they collocate with other words. This example illustrates how knowledge of collocations might be tested:

> **Look at the pairs of words printed in italics in the following text. In each case only one of the two words collocates correctly with the words before and after it.**
>
> > 3 One of the most charming and enduring images of the *ancient/antique* city of Cambridge – punting along the River Cam on a lazy summer afternoon – is quickly becoming one of the city's *biggest/largest* headaches. A dramatic increase *in/of* the number of tourists taking to the river is leading to traffic *lines/jams* on the Cam and a level of noise that is *bothering/disturbing* the peace of the university.
>
> Adapted from *Towards Proficiency – Student Book* by Peter May (Oxford University Press)

Although patterns of collocation are not easy to learn, they are an important feature of how language works and a strong argument for not learning words in isolation from their context. The following activity enables learners to practise such patterns.

 Collocations with *do, have, make,* and *take* – the class is divided into four groups, and each group given a dictionary. One of the four verbs, *do, have, make, take*, is assigned to each group. The students look up 'their' verb in the dictionary, and list ten common expressions which collocate with that verb. They then close the dictionary and write a sentence containing each expression. They can either write their sentences on an overhead transparency or whiteboard and present them to the class, or type them into a computer to create a gap-fill exercise for their classmates. The gap in each sentence should come directly after the verb, to elicit the expression which collocates with it in that context.

Knowledge of fixed expressions and idioms

Fixed expressions and idioms are collocations which are particularly strong and inflexible in form. Included under this heading are various types of fixed expression consisting of two or more words: compound nouns (*mobile phone, asylum seeker*), phrasal verbs (*the milk's gone off, I couldn't put up with her any longer, he turned down my offer*), multi-word units (*back to front, all at once, in a mess*), and idioms (*a pain in the neck, all fingers and thumbs, over the moon*).

Knowledge of main grammatical patterns and vocabulary

Exams tend to focus minds on the importance of grammatical accuracy: learners are explicitly penalized when they make grammatical errors in written answers, whereas little feedback on grammar may be received when they are using English for more communicative everyday purposes. Within the context of exam preparation, therefore, teachers and learners will probably give plenty of attention to consolidating knowledge of grammatical structures and how to use them.

Awareness of style and register

By the time they reach CEF levels C1 and C2 (ALTE levels 4 and 5), learners are expected to have developed some sensitivity to differences of style and register. Candidates may be asked to comment on a text writer's reasons for using a particular language feature, or the effect it creates on the reader. Summary writing, which may be required at level 5, also demands skill in adapting language to an appropriately neutral or formal style.

The connotations of words and phrases

When using a language in which they are fluent, people generally choose their words with care, intending to express particular feelings or ideas which would not be similarly conveyed if a different and more neutral word was used. These additional meanings are the 'connotations' of words. Learners need to develop an appreciation of what a particular word means in a particular context, and why that word rather than another has been chosen. In the TOEFL exam, for example, candidates are asked to choose the word which is closest in meaning to a word used in a reading passage.

> The word "serum" in line 3 is closest in meaning to
>
> (A) ointment
> (B) antitoxin
> (C) blood
> (D) acid
>
> From *Cambridge Preparation for the TOEFL Test* by Jolene Gear & Robert Gear (Cambridge University Press)

Learners of English are tested not only on the accuracy of their use of language but also on their range. The more awareness they develop of the connotations of different words and phrases, the richer will be the range of active vocabulary they can draw upon in descriptive writing and the more precisely they will be able to express what they are trying to say.

Connotation is related to collocation, since the connotations of particular words often determine whether or not they form appropriate collocations with other words. Here are some sentences from an exciting story told by a woman who survived a near-disaster during a canoeing trip along a river. In each case, one of the two words in italics has a more dramatic effect than the other, which makes it more appropriate to the context being described. Students are asked to think about the particular connotations of each word which produce this effect.

> 1 The boat *spun/went* into the bank.
> 2 The water was *dark/murky*.
> 3 I was *pulled/sucked* under the water.
> 4 I *tried/struggled* to hang on.
> 5 I *hauled/pulled* myself up.
> 6 All I could hear was the *noise/roaring* of the water.
> 7 Then, to my *great/inexpressible* relief, I heard a shout.
>
> From *New Proficiency Gold Coursebook* by J Newbrook & J Wilson (Longman)

Helping learners get to grips with grammar and vocabulary

There are some important teaching principles to bear in mind when helping students prepare for tests of grammar and vocabulary. Building on what students already know, teachers can get students to work out the rules that govern grammatical and verbal forms, and also encourage the use of learners' own errors to support learning. For grammar and vocabulary to be understood, teachers should draw attention to the use of language in context. While we want to train students to become independent learners, we can also make sure that they have the right exam techniques, so that they can approach any tests of grammar and vocabulary with confidence.

Building on what students already know

Few things are less motivating than being taught something that you already know, and students can find it stressful and frustrating to be taught by a teacher who assumes that there are lots of things that they do not know. Teachers should generally avoid starting grammar and vocabulary lessons with a formal presentation – as if it were being taught for the first time – of the language point to be practised.

On the other hand, students beginning an exam course need to understand that correct use of grammar and vocabulary is an important element in the assessment of their language ability and that, even if they have previously been taught something, this is no guarantee that they have learnt to use it correctly. Many students expect exam courses to highlight the teaching of grammar and vocabulary, and view this as an attraction; what they may be less prepared for is the responsibility of developing their ability to be accurate and to learn from their own mistakes.

A good starting point is to ask students how they think they learn grammar and vocabulary best, what they find most difficult, and what they think it is most important to learn. The information that we gather from this about students' own approaches to learning grammar and vocabulary will help us to plan future work, both for the classroom and for individual study. These consultations may well highlight ideas that we were already intending to use, as well as making us aware of activities that the students dislike, and differences between our own preferred approach and theirs.

Getting students to work out the rules

Grammar is easier (and more enjoyable) to learn if it is treated as something to be investigated and discovered. Students should already be familiar with the main terminology of grammar – the names of the different tenses, modals, articles, conditionals, reported speech, the passive etc – and they should also be able to recognize examples of the various forms and structures they denote. Grammar practice tasks should involve the students themselves in explaining why and how particular forms are used, what meaning they convey, and how certain pairs of sentences (although very similar in form) differ in meaning.

Vocabulary is better remembered when students are working with a mix of known and unknown items, and when words and phrases are organized in groups of related items. This relationship may be one of topic (e.g. natural disasters: *flood, earthquake, hurricane, drought*), meaning (synonyms and antonyms), form (phrasal verbs, prefixes, and suffixes), function (linking words, prepositions) etc. Research has shown that vocabulary must be encountered at least seven times before it is truly learned, and that it is easier to remember things we have engaged with actively and built relationships with. Familiar and unfamiliar vocabulary items therefore need to be practised together, discussed, and personalized in a variety of different ways, to be made memorable to the learner.

Students can work in pairs or groups on exercises which test their knowledge about the language, pooling ideas and working out their answers together. If the teacher is following an exam coursebook they will probably find that there are many grammar and vocabulary tasks which lend themselves to pair work, encouraging learning through personal discovery and shared knowledge. On the left are two examples of tasks which students can work on together to deepen and make explicit their understanding.

This sort of learning is much more likely to stick than if the teacher simply goes through the exercise, explaining each point as they go along. It is a mistake for students to believe that they learn more when the teacher is telling them what is correct than when they are discussing and thinking about the language point for themselves. Also, this is the time when the teacher can walk around, answer questions from individuals, monitor what the students are doing, and see who is having problems with the exercise.

Another effective approach to reviewing language is to get learners to create their own exercises to test themselves and each other. Here are some ways of doing this:

From *First Certificate Gold – Student Book*
by Richard Acklam & Sally Burgess (Longman)

■ Divide the words in the box into two groups, countable and uncountable. If there are words which you think can be both countable and uncountable, decide what the difference in meaning is between the two.

apple	wood	bread	travel
flu	furniture	iron	
headache	information		
business	chicken	luggage	
coffee	advice	country	
news	weather	chocolate	
hair	trip	work	cold	toast
fruit	equipment	rubbish	

■ Look at the following sentences and decide why each one is wrong or unlikely.

1 He's got a short, black hair and a beard.
2 I'd like a chicken to start with, please.
3 The news are very bad, I'm afraid.
4 My trousers hasn't been cleaned yet.
5 Let me give you some advices.
6 The police was very helpful.
7 Can I have another bread, please?
8 Let's go for a walk in a country.
9 I'd like to make toast to the bride and groom.

Students go through their notebooks and make a set of wordcards. On one side of each card they write a word or phrase that they want to remember, and on the other side a definition (in English) and an example sentence. Working on their own, students can use these cards to test themselves on vocabulary. Working in class, in a group of three or four, students can test each other, taking turns. They can either (a) read out a definition and see if anyone can guess the word, or (b) read out the example sentence, leaving a gap for the word that is being tested, and see who can fill in the missing word.

 Students work individually. For homework they choose eight words or phrases that they have difficulty using, and prepare eight sentences using them. They hand these in to the teacher for checking. In a follow-up lesson, the students work in pairs and dictate their eight sentences to each other. If noise is not a problem, it can be fun to get students to dictate to a partner sitting some distance away from them across the room, so that they have to speak the words loudly and with confidence. With everybody dictating at the same time, the energy level rises tremendously although the noise can be deafening!

Using learners' own errors

Students need to be made aware of the importance of monitoring their own language for errors. This is necessary, not just so that mistakes are noticed and corrected before work is checked by the teacher, but also so that when it is returned they can learn from their mistakes. It can be constructive for teachers to mark written work using a correction code which encourages the learners to notice and correct their own errors, rather than depending on the teacher to do this for them (see Chapter 4 for more on this). Students' own errors should also be a focus of individual study on those areas of grammar and vocabulary that are presenting particular difficulty for an individual. Teachers should provide guidance on what those areas are.

There are many different ways in which learners' errors can be used to design classroom activities that provide remedial practice in areas of common difficulty, and do so within the framework of a 'fun' lesson. Here are some of them:

 The teacher makes a collection of ten to fifteen sentences containing errors from students' homework and writes them on the board. Leaving a set of pens and a board rubber by the display, the teacher sits down quietly and allows the students to get up and correct the sentences. If the teacher can resist making any comment until the students have corrected everything they can, this gives an opportunity to observe the classroom interaction, while the class members discuss the sentences and advise each other on where and what the errors are and how they should be corrected.

The teacher prepares a set of ten sentences reflecting frequent student errors. The set should be prepared in two editions, each with five of the sentences written correctly and five written incorrectly (so, if sentences 1, 4, 5, 7, and 9 are correct on edition A, these five sentences are incorrect on edition B, and vice versa for the other five sentences). In pairs (where one student has edition A, and the other, edition B), and without showing each other their papers, the students read out their versions of each sentence and decide which is correct.

 A fun way of calling attention to grammar is to have a 'grammar auction' where supposedly correct sentences are 'sold' to the highest bidder. Students are given a set of fifteen sentences which include some that are correct and others that have mistakes in them. The mistakes should not be too obvious otherwise the game does not work. Class members are told that they have 5,000 euros which they *must* spend at the auction and that their aim is to buy as many correct sentences as possible. They prepare in groups, deciding which of the sentences are correct and therefore worth buying, and how much they are prepared to risk on each one. The auction then proceeds (for a full description of how to run a grammar auction, see Rinvolucri's *Grammar Games* (CUP)).

 The teacher can organize a language quiz. This takes quite a lot of preparation, in order to provide several sets of questions, testing different areas of grammar and vocabulary such as tenses, phrasal verbs, idioms, time expressions, uses of the article etc. There should be about ten questions in each category. Students are arranged in teams. Each team picks a category and nominates a team member to answer the question. If they cannot give an answer, the question passes to the next team and may be answered by the first person to raise a hand. If they get it wrong, it passes to the next team, and so on. Questions can be of various kinds, including the following:

- give me a sentence which includes the phrasal verb 'X'
- explain the difference between tense X and tense Y
- when is it possible to use X to refer to Y (e.g. past tense to refer to future time)?
- correct the following sentence: ......
- give me a way of joining these two sentences together into one sentence: ....
- give me an idiom using the word X and tell me what it means

Drawing attention to the use of language in context

Apart from practising grammar and vocabulary in free-standing exercises such as those described above, students can also learn how English works by looking at how words and phrases are used in longer pieces of text. Authentic or semi-authentic texts such as letters, magazine articles, transcripts of interviews and talks etc. can be studied, not only as reading or listening comprehension practice, but also to highlight particular features of language use. Students can be asked to look through a text and find examples of a particular grammar point, word, or phrase in use. Transcripts of listening material, as well as reading texts, can be used for this purpose. Having done it a few times in class, students can look for suitable texts themselves and prepare exercises with both comprehension questions and questions on the meaning and use of grammar and vocabulary items. They can then exchange their exercises with classmates.

Training students to become independent learners

When the pressure is on and classroom time is limited, as it often is in exam preparation courses, students need to understand the importance of studying on their own between lessons. Depending on the age of our students and how mature they are, this self-study can take the form of either set homework or encouragement to do additional work on areas of difficulty which they choose for themselves. Since grammar and vocabulary work is often remedial and widely catered for in self-study materials, it is ideally suited to individual study.

Early in the course, it is a good idea to spend some classroom time discussing with the learners how they can help themselves to improve by studying on their own, and to look at the use of dictionaries, grammar reference books, and self-study exercises. With good advice at the start, and monitoring of the amount and type of work that they do outside class, it may be more productive to encourage individual students to organize their own self-study time than always to set the same homework for everyone to do. If a more flexible approach is adopted, however, students should be given guidelines as to what is expected, and recommendations on what to do. They should be encouraged to keep a record of their self-study activities, containing information such as what materials they have used, how long the work took them, and whether or not the activity was (a) useful, and (b) interesting. They should have an opportunity to speak regularly with the teacher about their self-study activities.

Making sure that students have the right exam techniques

Finally, teachers need to give learners sufficient practice of exam-type questions, in exam-like settings, so that they know exactly what to expect on the day of the exam and are not surprised by anything unfamiliar.

Firstly, they need to be thoroughly familiar with the task rubrics. A surprising number of candidates lose marks because they do not do what is required. Examples of this are putting two words into a gap where only one word is allowed, or changing the form of the key word in a sentence transformation task.

Secondly, students need to recognize what the examiner is looking for in a particular question. In order to do, say, a sentence transformation correctly, the candidate needs to recognize which language point is being tested. Consider the examples on page 76.

> 1] It's very easy to maintain contact with friends nowadays.
> **touch**
> It's very easy .... with friends nowadays.
> 2] You missed the bus because you left home too late.
> **caught**
> If you had left home .... the bus.
>
> From *New First Certificate Gold Exam Maximiser*
> by Burgess with Newbrook and Wilson (Longman)

The first item may be a trap for candidates who try to use *touch* as a verb rather than recognizing that the required expression is *to keep/stay in touch with*. To complete the second item correctly, the candidate must be able to produce the conditional form *you would have caught*, and must also add the word *earlier* to complete the meaning: *If you had left home earlier, you would have caught the bus.*

Thirdly, candidates need to practise writing their answers on a separate answer sheet, making sure that the intended answer is clear and easy to read. Exam boards make strenuous efforts to give the candidate the benefit of the doubt when an answer is unclear, but they will not accept two alternative answers to the same question, nor may examiners be happy to wade through large quantities of crossed out work. Students need to know that spelling is taken into account in questions which test grammar and vocabulary and which, for the most part, have relatively short answers.

Lastly, candidates should understand that they may answer the questions in any order as long as the question numbers are clearly written on the answer sheet. It is generally a good idea to advise students to begin with a question they know they can do well, because by the time they have completed that they will have settled into the exam and be able to cope with the more difficult ones. However, candidates must resist the temptation of spending too much time on a question they feel comfortable with, at the cost of devoting insufficient time to less favoured questions. They must learn to manage their time and know how long to allow for each of the sections on the paper (and how the available marks are divided between those sections, where relevant). This can be difficult when there are a number of sections testing different types of language knowledge and requiring different amounts of time to complete. Practice exams can be very helpful here – as well as with many other aspects of exam technique.

Conclusions In this chapter we have:
- made some general points about the way that grammar and vocabulary are typically treated in an exam course syllabus.
- looked at some different sorts of tasks that can be used to test knowledge of grammar and vocabulary.
- drawn attention to accuracy and appropriacy as core concepts in assessment of language use.

- analysed the sorts of knowledge that are measured and assessed, which are: collocations, fixed expressions and idioms, the main grammatical patterns of English, connectors and linking expressions, awareness of style and register, word families, and the connotations of words.
- suggested some principles for teaching grammar and vocabulary for exams.
- advocated teaching approaches which enable learners to work out for themselves how the language works.
- pointed out that knowledge of grammar and vocabulary can be enhanced by study of its use in context, as well as in formal exercises and practice tasks.
- highlighted the need for students to develop good independent study habits.
- recognized the need for students to be thoroughly familiar with certain exam techniques and procedures.
- pointed out that much depends on familiarity with the format and intention of particular question types, and on recognizing which language point is being tested.

How to teach listening for exams

- Testing listening
- What kinds of listening tasks are there?
- How listening tests are conducted
- What is assessed in listening tasks?
- Developing task awareness
- Developing listening skills and strategies
- Building confidence and managing stress
- What do students need to remember in the test itself?

Testing listening

The skill of listening is usually tested by having candidates listen to audio recordings and complete written tasks to show their understanding of the spoken English that they hear.

There are several features of this activity which make it very different from most of the listening we do in real life. Firstly, in the real world listening is not an isolated skill but is part of social interaction. We can often interrupt when we do not understand or have lost the thread of what is being said, or when we feel we have listened for long enough and want to say something ourselves. We make sense of what we hear by putting it into the context of what we know about the topic, the speaker, or the situation. Secondly, in the real world we usually have control over what we listen to and when we listen. Whether or not we decide to pay attention to other people's speech is determined by our own needs and interests. Thirdly, in the real world – with the exception of radio and telephone communication – there are usually visual clues which help us understand what we are hearing; in face-to-face situations, if we can see the speaker, we pick up information from their gestures and facial expressions, as well as from their words. When we are watching a television programme or film, we have images to help us understand what we are hearing. Finally, other than when taking down messages or taking notes in a lecture, we don't usually respond to what we hear by writing something down, and we rarely answer questions about what we have just heard.

Although exam boards now base their listening material on the sorts of situations we are likely to meet in real life, it is probably impossible to create truly authentic listening tasks or, given the pressures and artificiality of the exam setting, to arouse much genuine listener interest in the topic or activity. Also, there are constraints on the number of times that the material can be heard. These factors can make listening tests a daunting prospect for students, so it is important not only to give them lots of practice before the exam, but also to build up their confidence by making sure that they are armed with strategies which are likely to lead to success.

Text types

Exam boards aim to make their listening material as authentic as possible, reflecting the different ways that the spoken language is normally used. Nevertheless, most listening material used in exams is scripted, and may sometimes sound 'unnatural'. When Tricia Hedge asked a group of teachers to compare the characteristics of natural conversation between native speakers with those of conversation scripted for the purpose of providing listening material for English language learners, the teachers came up with the following differences:

Spontaneous, informal speech	Recordings for language learners
• variations in speed of delivery, often fast	• slow pace with little variation
• natural intonation	• exaggerated intonation patterns
• the natural features of connected speech, e.g. elision	• carefully articulated pronunciation
• variety of accents	• 'Received Pronunciation'
• any grammatical structures natural to the topic	• regularly repeated structures
• colloquial language	• more formal language
• incomplete utterances	• complete utterances
• restructuring in longer, more complex sentences	• grammatically correct sentences
• speakers interrupt or speak at the same time	• speakers take careful turns
• speakers use ellipsis (i.e. miss out parts of sentences)	• ellipsis infrequent (i.e. sentences usually complete)
• background noise present	• background noise absent

From *Teaching and Learning in the Language Classroom* by Tricia Hedge (OUP)

Some of these observations about specially recorded material are now becoming somewhat less the case, certainly where exam listening material is concerned. For example, the recordings currently used reflect a variety of native and non-native speaker accents of English (though in mild, rather than strong, forms), rather than just Received Pronunciation, General American, or General Australian English. Features of spoken and colloquial language, such as incomplete sentences, hesitation, repetition, and use of idioms, are also common. Nevertheless, some of the characteristics listed by the teachers are fairly standard: only one person speaks at a time, probably a little slower than normal, there is little ambiguity in the message, and little distraction in the way of background noise. In addition, the text tends to have a clear beginning and end, and the language content may be limited, especially at lower levels, to make it easier to understand.

What kinds of listening tasks are there?

Task types

The kinds of tasks that are set in exams are often divided into two types, productive tasks and objective tasks. **Productive tasks** require a response which includes writing or correcting information. Examples of productive tasks include:

- note-taking, sentence or table completion
- short answers
- prompts with single words/short phrase answers
- identifying mistakes and correcting factual information

Objective tasks only require the learner to mark or circle the correct response. Examples of objective tasks include:

- Yes/No answers
- ordering information
- multiple choice
- True/False answers
- multiple matching

Candidates should pay close attention to the instructions given for each question, so that they are clear about what sort of response is required.

Themes and topics

Material used in exams is intended to relate to candidates' real-life concerns, needs, and interests. The texts chosen should be sufficiently broad in their content and appeal to provide a fair opportunity for all learners, whatever their background knowledge and culture, to be assessed on their listening ability. So the kinds of themes and topics used in texts for listening exams are likely to include:

- factual announcements, e.g. opening times, prices, telephone numbers etc.
- personal experiences and human interest stories
- announcements about events, the weather, local and international news
- travel and tourism
- leisure
- work
- the home
- sport
- science and technology
- environmental issues
- skills learning
- language learning
- popular culture
- popular psychology and social issues
- health

Usually, a narrator establishes the context, introduces the topic and describes the setting in which the spoken extract occurs, and this may help listeners to predict something of the content that they are going to hear. This introductory phase is also used to direct attention towards the relevant parts of the exam paper and reinforce what the candidate is expected to do.

How listening tests are conducted

The texts of listening exams are almost always pre-recorded, together with the candidate instructions. Professional actors with experience of this kind of work are used. Appropriate pauses are built into the recording, during which the candidates can read through each question before attempting the task, and check their answers afterwards. This means that, once the recording has started playing, it can be left running. Administrators check the recordings when they arrive at the exam centre, well before the exam, to make sure that there is nothing wrong with them. The quality of sound reproduction in the room where the exam will take place is also checked.

Most listening exams last thirty to forty minutes and have sections testing different types of listening. Time is allowed for the candidates to read through each question before they listen to the recorded text, and to check their answers after completing each section; in most cases these silent gaps are incorporated into the recording itself. In addition, it is now quite common at the end of the exam for candidates to be required to transfer the answers they have written on the question paper to a separate answer sheet which is computer-marked. Candidates need to be aware of these procedures and of the time allowed for transferring their answers. It is also worth pointing out to students that they should always answer while they are listening, rather than attempting the considerably harder task of trying to recall what they have heard so as to answer the questions afterwards.

The listening material for each section is usually, though not always, heard twice. Exceptions to note are the Cambridge ESOL Certificate of Advanced English, where Part 2 is only heard once, and the IELTS and Michigan examinations, where all parts of the listening test are heard once.

What is assessed in listening tasks?

Listening tasks are designed to assess the candidate's ability to process different forms of spoken English. The learners demonstrate their understanding by responding to a variety of tasks, which are similar to those encountered in the real world and depend on an accurate understanding of what is heard. The kinds of abilities tested include:

- locating and understanding specific information
- understanding detail
- understanding the overall message, or gist, of what is being said
- recognizing or inferring the speaker's attitude or emotions
- identifying genre, e.g. recognizing an advertisement, a voicemail message, a formal meeting etc.
- recognizing the topic of a conversation
- following the development of an argument or narrative
- matching spoken to written information
- following instructions or directions

Most listening exams consist of a series of about four different and unrelated tasks. The tasks involve a mix of long and short texts, and of monologue and dialogue. Here are some examples:

1 The candidate hears a series of short exchanges between interacting speakers, of about thirty seconds each. The task is to identify the relationship between the speakers, where they are (location), or what they are talking about (topic).

2 The candidate hears a monologue lasting about three minutes, such as a talk or a lecture. The task is to identify key pieces of information presented by the speaker.

3 The candidate hears a series of short monologues, each describing a different witness account of the same event. The task is to match each extract to a picture.

4 The candidate listens to a three-minute extract from a radio discussion between two or more speakers about a social or environmental issue. The task is to answer multiple choice questions about the different speakers' opinions and attitudes.

Answers are usually in the form of ticks and crosses, numbering of items, or completing notes or sentences with one to three words. Students should know that they do not have to give longer answers and that if they do they may even lose marks.

Developing task awareness

Students often experience listening exams as difficult. It is therefore important that classroom listening practice allows them to enjoy a high level of success and build their confidence from the start. An important aspect of preparation for listening tests includes developing awareness of the tasks involved, and knowing what to expect in the exam. With this in mind, some teaching ideas and approaches follow, along with sample lesson tasks which show how these work in practice.

Exam format

It is a good idea to let students know, early on in their course, exactly what the listening exam consists of and how long it is. It is better that they should be concerned about the reality of what is ahead than worry about ill-founded rumours. They should know:

- how long the exam is.
- how many tasks they have to do.
- what the various tasks are like.
- what sorts of answers they will be expected to give.
- how often they will hear the recording.
- where the exam will take place and how it will be conducted.

Whether or not it is wise to do a practice exam at this early stage will depend on the level of the students. If the preparation time is limited and they are not too far below the target level, trying real exam tasks can be a confidence-booster. On the other hand, if exposure to a mock exam is likely to scare learners and leave them feeling anxious, it is best not presented until much later in their preparation.

Task rubrics

The context and task are established by means of a rubric at the start of each section. This rubric normally contains clues to the content of what the candidate is about to listen to and instructions for what they have to do. Preparation time is allowed at the start of each section for the candidate to read through and make sense of the task.

Students need to learn the importance of using this time and information to get into the right frame of mind. The focus of the task may be on general understanding, specific points of information, speakers' opinions, attitudes or feelings, or some other feature of the discourse, while the rubric provides clues to context and situation. It is a good idea to provide practice in listening to and reading task rubrics. Students can answer true/false questions about the rubrics, highlight key words, and/or predict vocabulary they are likely to hear. Many coursebooks include these kinds of activities; an example is shown on the left.

> You will hear part of a radio programme about a young man who has become a celebrity because of his job.
>
> 1 First, look through the following gapped sentences to get a general idea of what the programme is about. What topics do you think will be discussed?
>
> The well-known chef, Jamie Oliver, was brought up in **(1)** .... in the country.
>
> Jamie started to help prepare meals at the age of **(2)** ....
>
> In London, Jamie met his future wife, Jools, who was working as a **(3)** ....
>
> Jamie appeared briefly in a **(4)** .... about The River Café in London where he was working.
>
> The recipes in Jamie's first TV series were **(5)** .... but used good ingredients.
>
> Jamie's food was popular because it matched the **(6)** .... of his trendy young audience.
>
> Both Jamie's TV series and his **(7)** .... were very successful.
>
> Jamie helped to prepare the food for the guests at his **(8)** ....
>
> Jamie then opened his own restaurant and trained **(9)** .... and inexperienced teenagers.
>
> Apart from cooking, Jamie enjoys playing the **(10)** .... in a band with his old schoolfriends.
>
> 2 Now look at the gaps in each sentence. Which gap(s) could be filled by:
>
> a) a number?
> b) a noun describing a place?
> c) a noun describing a job?
> d) an adjective describing food?
> e) the name of a musical instrument?

From *New First Certificate Gold – Student Book* by Jacky Newbrook, Judith Wilson & Richard Acklam (Longman)

Types of listening

Writers of listening exams design tasks so that they test a variety of different types of listening – long and short extracts, monologues, and dialogues – as well as choosing language spoken in a range of contexts and situations. The fact that exams test different sorts of listening may be of interest to students, and may help them to identify which sorts of listening they find easier and more difficult, and why.

To raise our students' awareness of this variety and

the different demands it makes, it can be useful to introduce a discussion of where and when they might hear spoken English, and what makes it easier or more difficult to understand. Here is a questionnaire that can be used to get the discussion rolling, or as a basis for designing our own:

1 **Would you expect to hear the following (a–l):**
   i) on the phone?
   ii) on a public address system?
   iii) on television or radio?
   iv) in a situation where you and the speaker are in the same physical space?

   a) Can you lend me 50 cents?
   b) We can't come to the phone at the moment, but if you'd like to leave a message, please speak after the tone.
   c) Hi, Sonia! How are you? You look fantastic.
   d) The train on platform four is a Wimbledon Line train, stopping at all stations to Wimbledon.
   e) Now it's over to Christy Spivak in Dar es Salaam.
   f) Could you put me through to the accounts department?
   g) Go straight down here until you get to the traffic lights and then turn left. Keep going and you'll see a church about four hundred metres down on your right. The tennis courts are just behind the church.
   h) That was Coldplay with their 2001 hit, 'Orange'.
   i) Excuse me. Is this seat taken?
   j) Passengers are reminded not to leave their baggage unattended.
   k) If you are inquiring about your most recent bill, press 1. If you want information about services, press 2. If you are reporting a technical fault, press 3.
   l) In this morning's lecture, I want to examine some of the causes of the Depression of 1929, but to do that I will need to go back to some of the points we made about the First World War.

2 **In which of the four situations do you find it easiest to understand what people say? Why?**

3 **In which situations are you expected to respond in some way?**

4 **Would you be expected to respond:**
   i) by writing something down?
   ii) by saying something?
   iii) by doing something?

Students should be encouraged to listen to as much spoken English as possible on the radio, television, or films and – if they are in an English-speaking environment – on trains, buses, public places, and anywhere that they can hear it spoken naturally. They can also be asked to do interviews with speakers of English and these recordings can be used in class to supplement exam listening material (see below).

Completing written answers

As mentioned earlier, in listening exams candidates generally write their answers directly on the question paper and then transfer these answers onto a special answer sheet at the end of the exam. It is important that teachers explain this procedure and give students plenty of practice with it. Although the invigilators at the exam centres usually check that students know how to complete the administrative parts of the answer sheet, the experience of doing the listening test will be far less stressful if students are thoroughly familiar with what they have to do. It is a good idea to use examples of the answer sheets in class in the last fortnight before the exam. Many published exam practice books provide examples of these.

Admittedly, misspelt answers are not normally penalized in exams designed to test listening, as long as the learner's meaning is clear and the mistake is a reasonable one for their level. However, in sentence-completion or gap-fill tasks students should check that their answers are correctly spelt and that they fit grammatically.

Developing listening skills and strategies

Although much of the general listening work we do with our students will help them prepare for the listening section of an exam, there are certain skills and strategies which relate directly to the exam itself.

Prediction

Research has shown that native speakers, when they listen, use their perception of the key features of context and their knowledge of the world to limit the range of possible utterances they are about to hear. Based on our existing knowledge and experience, we can predict that many listening situations will follow certain well-established routines or 'scripts'. For example, in a typical radio phone-in script, the presenter will check whether a particular caller is on the line, the caller will respond and greet the presenter, the presenter will return the greeting and invite the caller to make a comment, the caller will make their contribution and perhaps engage in some discussion with the presenter and other callers, and this will continue until the presenter thanks the caller and terminates their contribution. Examples of other scripts would be a voice message giving information about train times or cinema programmes, a conversation between doctor and patient, a job interview, and a speech welcoming new students to a school.

Almost all listening activities designed for language learners have a pre-listening stage in which a context and reason for listening are established before the text is played to the students. An introductory rubric fulfils this function for each section in listening exams. Even so, not all students switch automatically from passively reading through the rubric and the task instructions, into actively preparing themselves to listen by making predictions about what they are going to hear; so it is a good idea to pay some attention to this in the classroom. An exercise such as the following, using the sorts of rubrics used in the exam they are preparing for, will alert students to how much they can find out about what they are about to hear even before listening to the text:

What predictions can you make from the following rubrics about:

a) the speaker or speakers?
b) the context of speaking?
c) the sorts of things that will be mentioned in the text?
d) the length and style of the extract?

What clues are you using to answer these questions?

You will hear an announcement about a change in transport arrangements. (CAE)

You will hear a radio interview with a university lecturer who was carrying out some research in a Third World country when a flood disaster struck. (CAE)

In this part of the test, imagine you are part of a tour group. You are visiting the Sears Tower, which is the tallest building in Chicago. Now you will hear an introduction to the tour. (Michigan ECCE)

You will hear a news report about a theft from a vehicle. (CELS Higher)

Listen to this girl talking about a book she has just read. What does she think about the book? Is it: A. inaccurate? B. depressing? C. too long? (FCE)

You will hear five people talking about experiences connected with school. (FCE)

Another way in which prediction skills can be useful is when the task involves completing sentences or filling gaps. The students' knowledge of how English is structured should enable them to anticipate what sort of answer is appropriate to the context and will fit grammatically with what is already given.

On page 87 is a sentence completion exercise from the IELTS exam (from a university lecturer talking to overseas postgraduate students who have recently arrived in Australia). It is possible to fill in the boxes with appropriate information, giving consideration both to meaning and form, even without listening to the text. Of course, our answers may not be the right ones, but the prediction process helps us to focus on what sort of information we will have to listen for, and what form our answer should take.

If we try this with our learners, we could suggest that they complete only half of the sentences, and then listen to see whether their prediction was correct. However, they need to understand that, as an exercise, the point is to practise the sort of prediction that is possible, not to guess correctly.

From *IELTS Practice Now* by Carol Gibson, Wanda Rusek & Anne Swan (Centre for Applied Linguistics in the University of South Australia)

Complete the advice below by writing NO MORE THAN THREE words in the spaces provided.

30. When you go out, remember _____

31. Don't keep _____ at home.

32. Don't let other people see you with _____

33. Carry your _____ with you at all times when away from home.

34. Never leave your car or bicycle _____

35. When you go out at night keep to _____

36. Only go out with people _____

37. While you are settling in, it is better to go out _____

38. Never get into _____

Focusing on key information

Many second language learners think that they need to understand every word of the recording. Our experience of learning a second language can somehow make us forget that this is not the way we listen in our first language. Listening to a language we know well, we take notice only of those bits of information which are essential for our understanding of the message. At the same time, we use contextual clues to work out what it is that the speaker is saying. Our memory capacity and concentration span are limited and they prevent us from taking in every word of what we are hearing. In addition, real-life listening is often disrupted by background noise or mumbled and unclear speech. Nevertheless, none of these, in moderation, stop us being able to listen effectively in our first language.

So students need to learn, first, not to worry if they do not understand every word of a text when they listen to it, and second, that the strategies they use for listening in their first language can also be applied to listening in a second language. These include not only prediction, but also the ability to make inferences: to perceive logical connections between different, and sometimes dislocated, pieces of information in the text and in the task that is to be carried out. It is important to be able to make inferences based on prior knowledge and general common sense. This skill distinguishes good listeners from less effective listeners who become embedded in determining the meanings of individual words.

An activity type that focuses on choosing key information to note down is **dictogloss**. Here is an example of how it might be used:

Example lesson

The teacher prepares or records a short, spoken passage (no longer than two minutes) on a topic that will interest the students, and introduces it through images or a spoken description of what they are going to hear. Some prediction questions are asked, then the passage is read or played once, while students listen and check their predictions.

The second time the passage is heard, students are to note key words and phrases, but they may only note a limited number of these (depending on the length of the passage, this can be between five and fifteen words or short phrases). The passage is then read or played again.

With the students working in groups, they next try to reconstruct the text by pooling their key words and their understanding of what they heard. Each group can write up their reconstructed text and compare it with the reconstructions of the other groups in the class. As a variation, half the class could write down only key verbs and the other half write down only key nouns. The reconstructed texts are then generated by paired students from the two halves of the class. In both variations, students finally compare their reconstructions with the original text, and note the gaps between the two.

Note-taking strategies

Note-taking tasks form a part of most listening tests. Here is an example:

> You will now hear a short news item. Fill in the gaps in the summary below with the correct **word or phrase** according to what you hear. The first one has been done for you as an example.
>
> The traffic accident in ...*(Example)*.....*Lidham*.............
>
> has caused the death of **(14)**......................... persons, and a
>
> further **(15)**......................... people have been taken to St.
>
> John's **(16)**......................... for treatment. The northbound

Adapted from *101 Helpful Hints for IELTS* by Gary Adams & Terry Peck (Adams & Austen Press)

Note-taking is an extremely useful skill for learners to acquire. Learning note-taking in English may improve their note-taking in their first language, and this is likely to have benefits for them educationally and professionally. Note-taking skills also help learners cope better with non-productive listening tasks.

Although people who are in upper-secondary and tertiary education probably take notes in their first language, or even in English, exam candidates who have not been studying recently may have rusty or non-existent note-taking skills. Even competent note-takers may experience difficulty with exam note-taking tasks because they are rather different from normal academic note-taking. The most obvious difference is that the listener cannot see the speaker or any other visual supports such as blackboard notes or projected slides. The texts heard are also far shorter than a typical lecture. Another important difference is that, instead of making their own decisions about what to note down, candidates must complete the notes provided.

Exam task writers are expected to make sure that items to note are evenly distributed throughout the text, but occasionally the answer to one question may come very soon after another. Likewise, there may be stretches of text, particularly at the beginning of the recording, in which there is no need for candidates to make any notes and this can be puzzling. The notes inevitably express the content of the script in a slightly different form, though the actual words that students are intended to use to fill the gap in the notes are always used somewhere in the script as well. Many students have trouble recognizing key information if it comes in a slightly different position in the text to the position suggested by the gapped notes. For all these reasons, note-taking tasks represent a challenge to most learners.

Plenty of note-taking practice, both of the general skill and of the specific strategies needed for the exam, is the key. The dictogloss technique described above is helpful, but a motivating variation we might want to introduce is getting students to produce or bring their own texts. In this way, we can encourage students to listen and take notes outside class as well. Even if we are not teaching in an English-speaking country, it is very likely that our students have access to some television and radio broadcasts in English. The Internet is also an extremely rich source. Students can be asked to listen to a news story and prepare a summary. They can be told to speak from notes for which a word limit has been established and the dictogloss technique can be used once again. Alternately, students can be asked to prepare their own note-taking tasks to accompany their summaries. If we have encouraged them to make recordings of interviews with native speakers, extracts of the recordings can also be used.

Most teacher's books and exam practice books include tapescripts and these can be exploited in a variety of ways to increase confidence with note-taking. The following techniques represent graded practice in identifying relevant sections of the listening text and gaining familiarity with the way in which the notes sometimes express the information in the spoken text slightly differently. In each case, the task would be preceded by some kind of pre-listening prediction activity.

First, students do the prediction task and then receive copies of the tapescript. They are asked to underline the parts of the script that they think contain the most important information, i.e. information they would want to take note of. Students compare their underlining, first in pairs and then with the rest of the group. Next, the teacher gives out the note-taking task and gets students to check how much correspondence there is between their underlining and the note-taking items. Results are finally compared and discussed in open class.

After the pre-listening task, students listen to the text and focus on the note-taking items. They complete any items they can from memory. The teacher gives out copies of the tapescript and asks students to underline the sections where the answers to the note-taking task can be found. They then turn the tapescripts face down before listening to the recording again and completing the notes. Students can correct their own work by referring to the tapescript.

The teacher prepares copies of the tapescript in which some of the information relevant to the note-taking task has been altered, for example, a couple of dates changed. After a pre-listening prediction phase, students get copies of the 'doctored' tapescripts. They listen to the recording as they follow the script, locating the places where it differs. To finish, answers are compared round the class, replaying the tape and pausing on the relevant sections.

 The teacher prepares a list of sentences from the tapescript that correspond to the note-taking items, but adds one or two sentences that do not occur in the tapescript. After the prediction phase of the lesson, students are given copies of the sentences and allowed time to read them through. They listen to the recording and determine which sentences do not belong to the tapescript. The sentence handout is returned to the teacher, who focuses the class's attention on the note-taking items. Students try to complete the items from memory, and finally by hearing the tape again so that they can check their answers.

 After the prediction task, students receive copies of a completed note-taking task in which some of the items have been completed incorrectly. (These can either be grammatically impossible or unlikely in terms of meaning.) Students study the completions and locate the answers they think are incorrect, giving reasons. Then the recording is played, so that students can correct the completions.

 After the prediction task, students receive the note-taking items, but these include some completed and some incomplete answers. They listen to check the completions and to answer the other items.

Appropriate answers

If students are expected to do more than choose between a limited number of options (e.g. A, B, C, and D), it is normally the case that students only need to write between one and three words in productive listening tasks. Those candidates who write more almost inevitably run into trouble. If students have had a lot of experience of conventional dictation, they may think that the more they write, the more successfully they are demonstrating their ability to listen and accurately record what is said. It is therefore very important to emphasize to them that it is not dictation skills but comprehension of key information that is being tested.

Even when students are aware that one- to three-word completions are required, they will still need practice with appropriate answers. They need to be reassured that they can use the actual words of the text and that they do not need to paraphrase. Teachers should also reassure them that any numbers can and should be written in figures and that spelling is only a major issue in very high-level exams or if an answer (e.g. a name) is spelt out letter by letter.

Several of the activities suggested above for developing skills of prediction and note-taking, may also be useful in developing a sense of what an appropriate answer is. Here is another example of a prediction activity that can help with this:

---

2   You are going to hear part of an interview with a brother and sister called William and Frances who are in their twenties.

Before you listen, read the sentences below very carefully and see if you can guess the kind of word or phrase which may be missing.

As you listen, try to fill in the missing spaces using a word or a short phrase. Don't worry if you don't understand every word – try to pick out the key information and fill in the gaps by using the main words. Check that what you write makes sense – even if you're not completely sure that you have understood everything.

William and Frances used to (1) .... a lot when they were young.

Why did Frances dislike William? (2) ....

What is the age difference between Frances and William? (3) ....

What did William not help with? (4) ....

What is William ashamed of? (5) ....

What has Frances come to understand since growing up? (6) ....

From *Richmond First Certificate Course Student's Book* by Diana Fried-Booth (Richmond Publishing)

Sound discrimination skills

Discrimination of individual phonemes, of sounds in connected speech and in terms of prosody and meaning, makes a vital contribution to all aspects of listening. English notoriously presents many learners with difficulties in terms of length and quality distinctions between vowel sounds. Fortunately, there is a large amount of material to help learners recognize and produce long and short pure vowels and diphthongs, often in the context of minimal pair practice, for example, getting students to hear the difference between *ship* and *sheep*, or *hut* and *hat*. Much can be done that is intrinsically motivating for students to help them recognize these distinctions – see, for example, the various games (phonemic bingo, noughts and crosses, snap, and collaborative poem writing) in Kelly's *How to Teach Pronunciation* (2000: 40–43).

Likewise, the following features of connected speech also represent areas of difficulty for many learners, even at intermediate and advanced levels:

• **assimilation** – a change in a speech sound so that it becomes more like another sound that comes before or after it (e.g the *n* in *in between* will be pronounced with bilabial /m/ because sound /b/ is also bilabial)

• **elision** – the omission of one or more sounds (e.g. *can't dance* in rapid speech is often pronounced /kɑːndɑːns/)

- **linking** – sounds at the end of words are linked to sounds at the beginning of subsequent words so that they are pronounced as a single unit (e.g. *a piece of cake* will be pronounced /əpiːsəvkeɪk/)

- **intrusion** – an extra consonant is added at the end of a word to link it to a following word that begins with a vowel (e.g. many speakers of English will introduce an /r/ between a word ending in a vowel and a following *and* or *or*, as in *polka or waltz*)

- **juncture** – a boundary between two sounds that allows us to distinguish between groups of words that contain the same sounds (e.g. *seem ill* and *see Mill*)

- **contraction** – learners are often familiar with contractions in print but can be less used to hearing and recognizing contracted forms (e.g. in 'You *shouldn't have* told her', the contracted form sounds like /juːʃədnəv/)

While there is some controversy about how much productive work teachers should do with these connected speech features, there is little doubt that receptive awareness will help learners considerably with listening.

 Kelly describes an approach to the teaching of elision which is likely to be relevant to exam classes and which can be readily adapted to the teaching of the other areas listed above. He suggests that students listen to video or audio recordings so as to locate instances of elision, calling out to the teacher to pause the tape each time they hear an example. They are then given transcripts and asked to underline the examples before comparing with their classmates. Kelly sums up the value of this kind of activity as follows: 'Practice lessons like this can be invaluable in helping students to decode rapid, connected speech. While we may not realistically expect all students to incorporate such features consistently into their own language, they are at least becoming aware of these features.' (Kelly, 2000: page 121)

Once again, published tapescripts can be used for these activities, though it is also motivating to use extracts from films. Many film tapescripts can·be downloaded from the Internet, thus saving teachers time in transcribing any extracts they decide to use. It is important to check that final editing has not involved cuts in the script, and that copyright laws are respected.

Clearly word and sentence stress also deserve considerable attention, both in terms of production and reception. When presenting new vocabulary, teachers should always mark word stress, either by using the ' symbol, as in most dictionaries, or drawing a small square above the stressed syllable (e.g e'xams or exâms). Work on sentence stress can be done using the same technique described above for elision, with students marking stresses in tape or film scripts and then comparing what they have underlined.

 Finally, it is important to draw students' attention to their innate ability to use contextual clues to predict and guess even those words they cannot immediately recognize in speech. One way of raising awareness of this is through an activity in which the teacher 'hums' quiz questions rather than actually saying the words. At first, the whole question is hummed; then the teacher introduces a content word, so that 'What's the capital of New Zealand?' would all be hummed except for 'New Zealand'. Students try to guess the complete question.

Recognizing attitudes and feelings

Students will also need specific practice in recognizing attitudes and feelings, as expressed in spoken language. These are perhaps aspects of the listening skill that present teachers with the greatest challenge. It may be hard to make explicit all the 'rules' governing how listeners recognize attitudes expressed in spoken language, but practice enables tacit knowledge of this to grow. Penny Ur in her book *Teaching Listening Comprehension* (CUP) states that this ability is something we acquire in our first language and then transfer to contexts in which we learn other languages. Here is what she has to say about the explicit teaching of 'signals' of attitudes and feelings: '... I do not think that these can be systematically taught in any detail: they are too many, too subtle, too dependent on individual variation. [...] In any case, most of the aspects of social behaviour we are concerned with here (outward manifestations of mood and attitude for example) are to a great extent international; if they were not we would be unable to understand and appreciate foreign films, books and plays.' (p.160)

Among these signals are the various intonation patterns which do not have a one-to-one relationship to particular attitudes. Because of the difficulties involved in teaching the signals, an effective approach is one in which learners are given plenty of practice and the opportunity to discuss their interpretations of examples of speech. The particular activities that Ur suggests are very similar to a task type that now forms a part of many listening exams, e.g. Cambridge ESOL First Certificate. This involves the use of thematically related but otherwise decontextualized short extracts in which listeners have to work out who is talking to whom, where, what their relationship might be, and what they are talking about.

 A helpful activity uses extracts, either from recorded films and television programmes or audiovisual material specially prepared for language teaching. The class is divided into two groups. One group watches the extract with no sound and tries to guess what the speakers said. This group is entirely reliant on gesture, facial expressions, and the positions of the speakers relative to one another. The other group hears an audio recording without seeing the images on screen. Members of this group are drawing solely on linguistic information in their efforts to work out the context, what is being said, and the role relationships involved. Of course, some of the conclusions they draw will be as a result of grammar and vocabulary, but they will also have to pay considerable attention to intonation, so will be hypothesizing about the attitudes that intonation patterns convey. Their hypotheses are confirmed, modified, and refined through discussion with the other group. This takes place before both groups watch the complete sequence (with pictures *and* sound) again.

Building confidence and managing stress

Students often perceive listening exams as stressful, as well as difficult. Sound preparation for listening tests includes building confidence and developing strategies for dealing with stress.

Overcoming the stress factor

The fact that we feel tired after listening for long periods of time to speech in a foreign language is evidence of how stressful it can be. Unfortunately, listening is sometimes poorly handled in classroom settings, with the result that many students are very anxious indeed about it. An essential part of our role as an exams teacher will be to help them overcome and deal with listening-related stress.

The stress factors inherent in a listening task are the result of what is known technically as **noise**. When noise is present in a communication system, not all the information being transmitted may be received by the listener, because of interference of some kind. This interference may be the result of *physical* noise, such as a car alarm going off or the crackles and hisses of poor quality sound reproduction. Alternatively, the interference with receipt of the message may be due to a momentary lapse in concentration – distraction by *mental* 'noise' – on the part of listeners, or their inability to recognize the word or phrase. When this happens, listeners must rely on context to reconstruct whatever was missed and this puts additional pressure on them, particularly in situations where there are no visual clues and no possibility of asking the speaker to repeat what was said (something speakers do repeatedly in normal conversation).

For the foreign language learner there is inevitably far more 'noise' than there is for the native speaker and there are many more gaps to be filled by context. When a great deal is at stake, as is the case in exam preparation classes and the exam itself, the stress factor increases further still.

The essential step in helping our learners to overcome the 'noise' problem is to convince them that some 'noise' is inevitable and that it will not detract from their overall comprehension of what is said. One technique is to actually increase the amount of 'noise' in listening material.

 We can present our students with a listening task of some kind (note-taking, gapped text, true/false, or multiple choice) and then obliterate parts of the text that are not relevant to the task by turning the volume down on the cassette player, talking over the top of some sections, or making some other kind of noise. Another technique is to use material slightly above our students' level, so that they have to learn to cope with more gaps and distractions. It is preferable to use material with some kind of visual support (video recordings are ideal). Instead of conventional listening tasks, students are asked only for a short summary of what was said. To make the production task easier we can – if we are in a monolingual setting and have a knowledge of their language – ask for the summary to be given in the students' first language.

Songs can also be used to persuade learners that they do not need to understand every word. Most students listen to music sung in English and are apparently unperturbed by words and phrases that they do not understand, still managing to enjoy and appreciate the song. Native speakers often have considerable difficulty transcribing song lyrics themselves. We can ask our students to tell us what their favourite English language songs are and, if possible, to let us have access to copies of the songs and the lyrics. The students can then prepare (with help, if necessary) multiple choice items beginning with phrases like: 'The essential message of "xxxxxxx" is ...', 'This song is about ...'. The song can then be played in class and the other students asked to choose between the alternatives and to discuss which is best. This is particularly empowering if the songs are not familiar to the teacher, but very popular among students.

Aside from the inherent stress factors, many students have, unfortunately, experienced failure in listening tests or even during classes. As a result, they may 'seize up' as soon as they see an audiocassette player. A state of extreme tension then increases the 'noise' problem and thus produces a vicious circle, in which students become so frightened that they cannot concentrate and therefore fail yet again to understand what is on the recording. Each subsequent failure increases the fear factor and makes success an ever more remote possibility. Much work, therefore, needs to be done in class to increase confidence and get students to relax. Here are some possible approaches:

- **Easy listening** – being aware that one is making progress really helps to boost confidence. It is often wise to ensure that in the early stages of the course most of the material we use is actually below our students' level. This will ensure a high success rate. We can even use material students have heard before, perhaps while doing the lower levels of the same course – although we should not, of course, mislead students regarding the standard they will be expected to work to in the exam. As our course progresses, the class can occasionally go back to listening material they heard at the beginning, so they can see how much easier they now find it.

- **Casual listening** – the objective here is to help students separate the idea of listening from the stressful context of the test. While students are doing individual writing work of some kind, we can get into the habit of playing songs as background music and (at a later stage) recordings of English-language radio broadcasts. We could start up a conversation with a student who finishes before the others or might even arrange for a colleague to drop into the classroom and chat to us briefly while they are working. There is no need to ask for comments or answers to questions at the time. If we like, in a subsequent class we can make some reference to what was said or played and see if anyone remembers it but, in fact, the activity has served its purpose without further exploitation.

- **Empowering listening** – here the aim is to increase confidence and motivation, by getting students to decide what *they* want to comprehend and respond to in the listening material. Ideally, this will be some kind of provocative literary text (a poem or a dramatic monologue, a song, or even an advertisement). Students are told that they can respond in any way they like, by writing down a couple of words or phrases, by drawing something, by writing another text. Anyone who wants to share their response is welcome to do so, but pressure should not be put on those students who are reluctant.

- **'We ask the questions'** – the aim here is similar to 'empowering' listening. Groups of students become 'experts' in relation to the listening material. They are given access to the transcript and prepare the task and manage the listening practice in class, making decisions about how often the recording is heard, checking the answers, and so on. Once again, student-produced recordings of native speakers can be used. All class members should have the opportunity of doing this.

- **Listening to relax** – there is a dual objective here: first to follow a step-by-step relaxation programme and secondly to listen to, understand, and follow instructions. There are innumerable accounts of relaxation techniques available in books and on the Internet; here is an example:

Deep Breathing

Deep Breathing is one of easiest stress management techniques to learn and the best thing about it is it can be done anywhere. When we become stressed, one of our body's automatic reactions is shallow rapid breathing which can increase our stress response. Taking deep, slow breaths is an antidote to stress and is one way we can "turn-off" our stress reaction and "turn-on" the relaxation response. Deep breathing is the foundation of many other relaxation exercises.

☹ Get into a comfortable position, either sitting or lying down.

☹ Put one hand on your stomach, just below your rib cage.

☺ Slowly breathe in through your nose. Your stomach should feel like rising and expanding outward.

☺ Exhale slowly through your mouth, emptying your lungs completely and letting your stomach fall.

☺ Repeat several times until you feel relaxed.

☺ Practice several times a day.

From the Stress Management web page at:
http://www.studhlth.pitt.edu

Most such accounts include deep-breathing, muscle-relaxation, and visualization exercises. We can explain to the students that developing familiarity with these will help them keep calm in the exams themselves. We thus provide an incentive for following the instructions and overcome resistance from those who would rather be doing another multiple choice cloze test! We read the instructions while the students perform the exercises. As a follow-up, we could provide them with a gapped-text task based on the instructions. Students see how many of the gaps they can fill from memory and then have the instructions read again for them to check their answers. In the above example, the parts of the text that might be taken out for the gap-fill task are circled.

What do students need to remember in the test itself?

It is also important to provide students (who may otherwise tend to get flustered) with coping strategies for the listening test itself. The following is a checklist for students to follow (much of this advice applies to other types of exams too, of course).

> **BEFORE THE TEST STARTS**
> 1 Have the right documents and equipment.
> 2 Get there in plenty of time.
> 3 Wait quietly and RELAX.

It may be stating the obvious, but they should be advised to check that they have their exam registration form, their identity documents, several pens and pencils, a rubber, and so on. They should get to the exam centre in plenty of time, but avoid waiting outside the door of the exam room and working themselves up into a frenzy by talking to other candidates. In most exam centres, students are not allowed to have contact with candidates who have already taken the test, so they should be told to wait quietly nearby and to practise some of the relaxation techniques they have learnt in class. In settings where English is not heard often, students might benefit from playing recorded versions of these on a personal stereo so as to 'tune into English' before the test itself.

> **IN THE EXAM ROOM**
> 4 Do what the invigilator tells you to do.
> 5 Read the instructions and the questions.
> 6 Don't speak once the recording has started.

In the exam room, candidates should follow the instructions given to them by the invigilator as regards filling in their personal information on the answer sheet, and so on. As soon as they are told to do so, they should read through the instructions, look at the questions, and try to make as many predictions as they can about what they are going to hear. If they want to, they can note these on the question paper. Students should understand that, in almost all cases, once the invigilator has started the tape it cannot be stopped and that they should not try to speak to either the invigilators or any of the other candidates.

DURING THE TEST

7 Note down key words and phrases.

8 If you miss an answer, go on to the next question.

9 Focus on missed answers the second time you hear the recording.

10 Use context and memory to help you work out any answers you missed.

11 Don't leave questions unanswered.

12 Check your spelling and grammar.

13 Transfer your answers.

14 Breathe a sigh of relief!

It is worth reminding students that they can write anything they like and as much as they like on the question paper, so if they want to note down words and phrases they should do so. The Michigan exams actually set aside space for this. They should also complete any answers they can manage on the first listening. If they miss an answer on the initial listening, they should make a mark on the question paper and immediately go on to the next question. If it is a task where the recording is only played once, they should try to complete the question using grammatical or contextual clues. If they hear the recording a second time, they should focus on the answers they missed, giving these priority. Once again, missed answers can be worked out from context or, in the case of non-productive tasks, guessed. No question should be left unanswered as this may lead to errors (such as skipping an answer and then filling in all subsequent answers in the wrong place) when completing the answer sheet. Finally, candidates should check spelling and grammar before transferring their answers. At the end of the test they should breathe a sigh of relief and give themselves a pat on the back. What, for many, is the worst part of the exam, is now over.

Conclusions

In this chapter we have:

- outlined the main features of listening tests.
- listed the major text types found in exams.
- reviewed the differences between spontaneous informal speech and scripted, recorded listening material.
- looked at the task types used to test listening comprehension.
- listed themes and topics commonly used in listening tasks.
- explained how most listening exams are conducted.
- looked at how specific abilities are measured in listening tests.
- suggested ways of developing task awareness in terms of exam format, task rubrics, types of listening, and completing answers.
- suggested ways of developing listening skills (predicting, focusing on key information, note-taking skills, appropriate answers, sound discrimination, recognizing attitudes and feelings, overcoming stress).
- provided a checklist of things to remember when taking the test.

How to teach speaking for exams

- **What kinds of speaking tests are there?**
- **How speaking exams are conducted**
- **What is tested in speaking exams?**
- **How to prepare students for speaking tests**

What kinds of speaking tests are there?

Traditionally, speaking tests have tended to consist of meetings between one candidate and one examiner (**one-to-one testing**). In this situation, the examiner has to do two things simultaneously: interact with the candidate and assess their performance. An alternative format, increasingly favoured by exam boards, has two (occasionally three) candidates enter the exam room together, with two examiners present (**paired testing**).

Students may expect one-to-one testing and perceive it to be fairer, since they worry about their performance being adversely affected by the presence of other students. However, there are advantages to the paired testing format, which candidates can be made aware of:

- It provides more authentic opportunities for interaction.
- It increases the range of task types that are possible.
- It enables two examiners to be present and to take different roles: one takes the role of **interlocutor** and the other the role of **assessor**. The interlocutor conducts the examination and interacts directly with the candidates. The assessor only listens and can therefore give full attention to how well each candidate is performing.
- Marking is more objective since two examiners grade the candidate's performance.

Typically, a speaking exam consists of a series of short tasks. Each task is designed to demonstrate a different function of the spoken language. Four different task types are common to most speaking exams. These are:

- Interview tasks
- Presentation tasks
- Negotiation tasks
- Discussion tasks

As the whole exam may last less than ten minutes at lower levels, and only twenty minutes at more advanced levels, the time allocated for each task is quite brief, so students should be prepared for the examiner to interrupt if they speak for too long. However, they should be encouraged to give more than one-word answers to questions, and to show what they are capable of.

Interview tasks

Nearly all exams begin with an interview or 'question and answer' task, which serves the dual purpose of settling the candidates and testing their ability to provide general personal information. They answer questions about everyday topics such as themselves, home and family, hobbies and interests, reasons for study, future plans etc. At lower levels, the questions require mainly factual answers and simple expressions of opinion; at higher levels, they demand greater reflection and ability to express ideas.

Examples of lower–level questions:

Where are you from?
Is that a town or a village? Is it an interesting place to visit?
Tell me something about your family. Have you got brothers or sisters?
What do you like most about learning English?
What are you planning to do when you finish studying?

Examples of higher–level questions:

In addition to languages, what other life skills do you think will be
   important in the 21st century?
Looking back on your education up to now, is there anything you would
   like to change?
Who has had the biggest influence on your life so far, would you say?
How ambitious are you?

In some exams candidates may be expected to ask the other candidate or the examiner questions based on prompts.

Example prompts for paired interviews:

I'd like you to ask each other something about:
   your reasons for learning English
   your future plans
   your feelings about the place where you live etc.

Presentation tasks

A presentation task is one in which a candidate has to speak at length, usually for between one and three minutes, on a prescribed topic. Examples of this type of task include delivering a prepared talk from notes, describing one or more pictures to another person, and giving instructions. The candidate is generally given a visual or verbal prompt around which to structure their presentation. A **visual prompt** might be a picture or set of pictures, a chart, or diagram.

Example of what the interlocutor may say in an advanced test:

I'm going to give you three photographs and ask you to talk about them for one minute. I'd like you to compare and contrast the photographs, commenting in particular on the relationships shown between people and animals. Please also say which of the three pictures you think is the most appealing, and why.

A **verbal prompt** will indicate a topic and perhaps provide a list of points to help the candidate to focus on suitable content and structure.

Example of what the interlocutor may say in an intermediate test:

I'm going to give you a card with a topic written on it. Read the card carefully. You will have two minutes to prepare what you are going to say about the topic and then I will ask you to speak for one to two minutes.

Or:

Describe a journey you have made when you met someone interesting. Where were you going? Who did you meet? What was so interesting about the person?

Presentation tasks are intended to show the candidate's ability to speak at length in an appropriately fluent and coherent manner. This kind of task demands different skills from those needed for simply asking and answering questions.

The range of topics likely to come up at a particular level can often be predicted. Some exam boards even provide in their handbooks a list of the topics on which candidates are expected to be able to speak. The following list, from the CELS Handbook, is used as a basis for exams at all levels:

- work
- fashion
- lifestyles
- the arts
- social development
- human emotions (e.g happiness)
- the media
- personal experiences
- relationships
- tastes
- education
- sport
- cultural norms / differences
- progress
- entertainment / leisure
- science and technology
- travel / tourism
- consumerism
- health
- society
- language learning

If we take each topic and start thinking of questions related to it, we soon begin to see the sorts of areas that emerge as material for presentations. For example, if the topic is 'work', the kind of questions candidates could expect might include the following:

> What sort of job do you do / would you like to do?
> What do you like most / least about your present job?
> What are the most important things that make a job good or bad?
> Are men and women capable of doing the same jobs, or are there some jobs that only men or women can do?
> Which jobs are most useful to society?
> Which jobs should earn the most money?

And the topics which they might be expected to talk about for a presentation could include:

> Tell a story from pictures about someone who had a really bad day at work.
> Describe your job, and say what you like most and least about it.
> Describe your ideal job. Give three reasons why you have chosen it.
> 'We are a sick society. Half of us are working much too hard, and half of us have no jobs at all.' Say why you agree or disagree with this statement.

Negotiation tasks

A negotiation task is one in which candidates discuss a given situation in order to reach a decision. They may be required to make suggestions, discuss alternatives, find differences, put items in order, or speculate about a situation.

Negotiation tasks are very popular group activities in ordinary language classes, and the kinds of collaborative task used in exams should be familiar to teachers and students who use group work. In paired testing, the interlocutor usually explains the task and then withdraws, leaving the students to discuss the situation with each other (the interlocutor may join in at a later stage – see Discussion tasks, below). In one-to-one testing, the interlocutor is involved as co-participant in the discussion and/or decision-making process. Usually, whether or not the speakers succeed in reaching a consensus is less important than their ability to demonstrate awareness of other points of view and negotiating skills in the tested language.

> **Example of a lower-level task:**
>
> A friend of yours has a birthday next week and you would like to give her a present. Here are some suggestions [*Interlocutor gives pictures to the candidates*]. Talk about the suggestions and then decide together which is the best present for your friend.
>
> **Example of a higher-level task:**
>
> I'd like you to imagine that you have been asked to write a magazine article about the problem of overcrowding in our towns and cities. Here are some pictures that might give you some ideas [*Interlocutor gives pictures to the candidates*]. You can choose two of them to illustrate your article. Decide together which of the pictures you will use.

Discussion tasks

Discussion tasks tend to form the final phase of a speaking exam, and to provide an opportunity for the interlocutor to intervene directly. The discussion topic is likely to link thematically with the earlier activities. The interlocutor introduces one or more open-ended questions to generate discussion with the candidate(s). This is the most complex of the four task types – candidates are expected to be able to articulate opinions and beliefs – but it is also a final opportunity to show themselves and their speaking abilities at their best.

> **Here are some example discussion topics at intermediate level:**
>
> How important do you think it is to learn foreign languages?
> What do you think is the best way to learn a foreign language?
> How do you think language learning methods are going to change in the future?
>
> **And some at advanced level:**
>
> Why do you think people create so much waste in the world today?
> How should we protect our environment from the effects of waste?
> Who should be taking action to reduce waste – the government or the people?

How speaking exams are conducted

Knowing what to expect in a speaking exam can go a long way towards dispelling the anxiety associated with entering the exam room. It is important that students know beforehand exactly what test procedure will be adopted and how the examiners will behave. It is worth finding out from the exam board whether they produce a video which can be shown to students, as candidates can then see for themselves what to expect, in terms of both exam procedure and the level of performance required.

Teachers should ensure that candidates are informed about and prepared for the following aspects of the conduct of exams: examiner behaviour, how paired testing is conducted, and the recording of speaking tests.

Examiner behaviour

Entering the exam room is a moment of tension for any candidate. Examiners understand this and will normally do their best to put candidates at ease by welcoming them and showing them where they should sit. The examiner will then introduce him or herself and any second examiner present, and ask candidates to introduce themselves.

All exam boards take great care to ensure standardization in the way that speaking tests are conducted and assessed. Many exam formats nowadays require the interlocutor to speak from a prepared script. While it may be disconcerting for the student to be interacting with someone following a script (it makes the test rather different from normal face-to-face communication), this standard format does mean that, no matter where the exam takes place, the candidate can be assured of being given the same chance as everyone else. As long as students know in advance that the interlocutors have to stick to predetermined wording, they should not be confused by their lack of spontaneity and the fact that they may look down at a paper from time to time.

When two examiners are present in paired testing situations, it is the usual practice for one examiner to be the primary assessor and take no part in the group interaction. For many candidates, the sight of someone in the corner who says nothing and makes notes can be terrifying, all the more so if they are not prepared for it. It is important that they understand that this person is not there to write down all their mistakes. What the assessor is doing is listening very carefully to what each candidate is saying, recording aspects of their performance in the light of the assessment criteria, and completing the required administrative information.

Examiners are responsible for managing the time available and are working to a fairly tight schedule. Students often feel, when they come out of an exam, that the time has gone much faster than they imagined, and that they did not have enough time to develop what they were trying to say. It is a good idea to prepare students for the fact that the examiner may sometimes seem to cut an activity short. They should understand that this is not a criticism of their performance but a response to time constraints.

At the end of the exam, the examiner will thank the candidate(s) and indicate that that it is time to leave. Although it can seem strangely formal, candidates should not˙expect any indication from the examiner about whether things have gone well or badly.

Conduct of paired testing

Since this may be a less familiar testing format than one-to-one testing, it is worth drawing attention here to some special features of the conduct of paired tests, especially now that this is an increasingly favoured format.

eir examination in pairs and are assessed on the quality of
with each other as well as with the examiner.
nistrators are not normally required to give advance
which students will be paired, so it is up to the teacher to
er it is beneficial for pairs to be decided ahead of the exam.
ge is that students can practise with a particular partner, and
noose who that partner will be (although pairing best friends
not always a good idea, as such a high degree of familiarity may
t they fail to produce as much language as they would with
they don't know!). A disadvantage is that if one member of the pair
urn up on the day, the pairings can fall apart as the examiners may
n seeing the candidates who turn up, in pairs, in the order in which
rrive to take the exam. If there is an uneven number of candidates on
ay, a group of three will often be formed at the end of the testing
on.

ome students will find the idea of doing their test with another learner
worrying. Even if they know their partner, they may feel shy about having
to speak in front of this person or worry that their partner will not give them
a chance to speak, will be too silent, or will affect their performance in some
other negative way. It is important for candidates to understand that,
whether or not they have met and practised beforehand, they can rely on the
examiners to make sure that they have their full allotted time to speak; and
that they are assessed as individuals.

Recording of speaking tests

Exams are sometimes recorded for monitoring purposes. This is particularly
important in one-to-one testing, where a test is taken by a single candidate
and assessed by just one examiner. It can be difficult for solo examiners to
arrive at a final assessment during the test itself because they have to give so
much of their attention to actually conducting the test, so it is fairer to enter
a final mark after listening to the tape. It also means that if there is any
dispute over the grade awarded, the recording can be checked again. Exam
boards may also require some exam sessions to be recorded for their own
monitoring systems.

The presence of recording equipment can be unsettling if learners are not
prepared for it. They should be warned that this may happen, and can be
given encouragement to record and listen to their own voice, before the test.
If they do not have access to recording facilities, or the teacher has no time
to organize such activities with the students, one easy method is to get
students to leave messages on their own telephone voice mail.

What is tested in speaking exams? Formal assessment criteria are laid down by the exam boards and are usually
available to schools and colleges preparing students for exams. Cambridge
ESOL (see the Exams overview) has developed a Common Scale of
Speaking as a general reference document for comparing all the types and
levels of speaking exams that it administers. A similar scale exists for the
Michigan exams. They illustrate how performance criteria may be defined,

and act as an indicator of the level of performance demanded at different levels of proficiency. Examiners refer to such scales and marking guides provided by their exam boards to assess the sub-skills tested. Typically, two sets of assessment criteria are used by examiners in paired testing situations: a scale of overall or global competence, and a scale of competence in particular sub-skills of speaking. The interlocutor only assesses globally, while the assessor uses both scales to determine the grade awarded.

Sub-skills tend to cover the following areas of language use, although the exact terminology varies from one exam to another:

- Discourse management
- Interactive communication
- Grammar and vocabulary
- Pronunciation

Discourse management (fluency and coherence)

Discourse management involves the ability to control language over more than a single utterance, and to express ideas and opinions in coherent, connected speech. It is tested primarily in **one-way tasks**. One-way tasks, as their name suggests, are tasks where the main communication is one way, from speaker to listener(s). Examples of one-way tasks include presenting, narrating, describing, instructing, explaining, predicting, or communicating a decision. (Two-way tasks are dealt with in the next section.)

Candidates at the lower levels are not expected to be fully **fluent** (i.e. able to speak over a period of several seconds without having to pause to summon language), but they should be able to continue speaking beyond a single utterance, albeit with some hesitation and searching for words. At higher levels, the candidate should be able to maintain an extended flow of **coherent** speech (i.e. speech in which ideas and concepts are logically connected and developed) which the listener can follow with ease and which shows a sense of the natural pauses, hesitation, and rephrasing of English mother-tongue speakers.

Interactive communication (turn-taking, initiating, and responding)

Interactive communication is the ability to engage in conversation or discussion. The main skills of interactive communication are appropriate turn-taking, initiating, and responding at the required speed and in the correct rhythm. It is tested mainly through **two-way tasks**. These involve at least two speakers, and tend to demand considerable negotiation and clarification of meaning. Problem-solving, negotiating, and discussion tasks, in which candidates share ideas and opinions with each other and/or with the interlocutor, are of this kind.

In two-way tasks, speaking turns tend to be short and typically people compete with each other for an opportunity to speak. **Turn-taking** (i.e. deciding when to speak, how long to speak for, and how to indicate that you are willing for someone else to speak) is a complex skill which mother-tongue speakers manage instinctively but non-native speakers sometimes have difficulty with. Although they may seem self-evident, turn-taking conventions do differ from one language and culture to another. If we have a multicultural group of students in our class, we can observe them speaking together in groups for a demonstration of this. In particular, different cultures vary in their tolerance of several people speaking at the same time, of people interrupting each other, and of pausing. Although turn-taking in the mother tongue is an intuitive habit and difficult, if not impossible, to change, it can cause native speakers of English to judge non-native speakers as shy or cocky, polite or impolite. So it is worth pointing out some basic principles of turn-taking in English:

- Only one person usually speaks at a time.
- Transitions from one speaker to another usually happen smoothly, without gaps or overlaps. When an overlap occurs, one speaker quickly gives way to the other.
- Pauses and silences are felt to be uncomfortable and tend to be filled as quickly as possible.

Part of what is assessed under interactive communication is candidates' ability to **initiate** interaction by asking questions, making suggestions, and so on. Students may be unused to doing this in English, particularly in the context of an exam. They will therefore need practice with the language and the management of initiation. It is worth playing some recorded examples of both successful and unsuccessful candidates interacting, to illustrate how vital this skill is and then to introduce some of the language involved (e.g. *Shall we start? What do you think? How about … ?* etc).

Candidates also need to learn to **respond** appropriately to what the other candidate says. They need to know whether a verbal response is required (sometimes a raised eyebrow, a smile, or a shrug may be enough) and what length and form that response should take. Sometimes 'minimal responses' (*Mmm, Really?, I see, Oh no!* etc) are more appropriate than a longer response that might be interpreted as an attempt to get a speaking turn. Minimal responses show that an interlocutor is listening to and taking an interest in what the other speaker says. They are therefore very important. They also vary considerably from one culture to another, both in terms of their frequency and, obviously, their form. It is worth providing students with some input on these minimal responses and encouraging their use in pair and group work.

Grammar and vocabulary

Range and accuracy in the use of grammatical and lexical forms are assessed at all levels.

Low-level candidates are expected to be able to use correctly a limited and often formulaic set of expressions, while avoiding excessive repetition.

Intermediate-level students should be able to demonstrate some spontaneity and variety in their language, although some inaccuracy and inappropriacy is expected and excused.

An advanced level of oral competence is indicated by the ability to use a wide range of vocabulary and grammatical structures in appropriate contexts, and to express precise meanings, attitudes, and opinions without resorting to simplification. As candidates take tests at higher and higher levels, they are, eventually, expected to show that they can correctly operate a range of resources which is little short of that available to an educated native speaker, and can maintain the direction and flow of the interaction without difficulty.

Pronunciation

Pronunciation is assessed in all speaking exams, in relation to both production of individual sounds and control of **prosodic features** (stress, rhythm, and intonation). While pronunciation teaching is increasingly incorporated into the syllabus of General English courses, it can be all too often overlooked among the many competing demands of preparing for exams and is rarely focused on in exam preparation materials, with the exception of those written specifically for exams in spoken English. Kelly's *How to Teach Pronunciation* (in this series), and the suggested exercises near the end of this chapter, offer some ideas for helping students prepare for this aspect of speaking tests.

How to prepare students for speaking tests

Preparing students for an exam in spoken English can present certain dilemmas which are less likely to occur in non-exam contexts. What kinds of speaking activities are most useful? How much time should be spent practising speaking skills when there are so many other exam skills to be practised? What can be done to build up the confidence of students who are terrified at the thought of having to speak English in the presence of an examiner?

To ensure that we are giving our students the best chance of performing well in the exam we should:

- make sure that we ourselves are thoroughly familiar with the 'what, who, and how' of the particular exam our students are preparing for (this will also help us to see just how far spoken language testing has moved towards simulating real communication, and to justify the authenticity of the activities we ask our students to do).
- make sure that candidates know exactly what to expect and what their particular strengths are in speaking.
- make clear how the speaking work done in class is designed to match the requirements of the exam and to build up the skills that candidates will be expected to demonstrate.

With respect to the first aim, the Exams overview and table at the back of this book should help teachers to be well-informed about exams they are dealing with. In order to develop teaching approaches which meet the last two of these aims, it is worth considering the various different aspects of speaking exams – their format, content, criteria, and the skills being tested.

How to make sure that students know what format the exam will take

From a teaching point of view, the fact that interlocutor scripts are used to standardize the conduct of exams opens up a range of possibilities for teachers to provide classroom practice which simulates the exam procedure.

Examples of examiner scripts, such as the one shown in the activity below, can be found in many exam handbooks. Students can practise in pairs or groups with one student taking the role of the examiner. Even quite low-level learners would be able to perform the role of examiner using the instructions provided in the script.

Putting learners in the interlocutor role greatly increases their understanding of the mechanics of the test, and familiarizes them with what the interlocutor is going to say in the exam itself. It also means that teachers can monitor a much larger number of learners practising together than they could if they were taking the role of interlocutor themselves.

Example lesson – understanding and practising the exam format

The script used here is for an exam in which candidates are tested in pairs, but the idea can easily be adapted for one-to-one testing.

Before class: the teacher finds an interlocutor script for the exam the students are taking (an example is given on page 110; but these scripts can be found in exam handbooks and teachers' book editions of practice tests). A copy is provided for each student in the class.

In class: The teacher starts by giving students information about the exam and this particular part of the speaking test. Students practise ways of comparing and contrasting images, since that is what this test task involves. With the class divided into groups of three or four, each group decides who will initially take on the roles of the interlocutor, assessor, and candidate(s). The interlocutors then receive their instructions and any necessary additional material (e.g. the visual prompts that go with the script). They go back to their groups and conduct the simulated test. Meanwhile the teacher circulates, monitoring the groups and noting any points for correction or comment. Once everyone has had a turn as candidate, the teacher leads a whole-class feedback session, writing up any language needing correction on the board, as well as examples of good use of the language of comparison and contrast.

How to prepare students to be examined in pairs

The more used students are to working in pairs or groups, the better. Many problems arise simply because students have not had enough practice at negotiating in English with a partner before they get to the final exam. It is also important to raise students' awareness of the features of a successful paired-task performance. Awareness-raising typically involves getting students to compare examples of people performing paired exam tasks, both very effectively and not very well. Watching and analysing a video of two candidates taking part in a speaking test would be a good way of doing this. For example, students can be given questions highlighting particular features of management of interaction such as the following:

• Which speaker(s) asked for their partner's opinion?
• Which speaker(s) only gave very brief answers?
• Which speaker(s) disagreed politely with what their partner said?
• Which speaker(s) developed a point their partner made?

INTERLOCUTOR INSTRUCTIONS

This is what you should say to your candidates. Do NOT show them this piece of paper. Give Candidate A the first two photographs and say:

[Name of Candidate A], these photographs show different kinds of houses. [Name of Candidate B] you can look at them too. We'll look at your photographs in a minute. [Name of A] I'd like you to compare and contrast these photographs, saying which house looks more attractive to you. Remember you have about a minute for this, so don't worry if I interrupt you.

Time Candidate A and say 'Thank you' after about a minute. Then say to Candidate B:

[Name of B] which of these two houses would you prefer to live in?

Say 'Thank you' after Candidate B has been speaking for about twenty seconds. Take the first two photographs back. Give Candidate B the other two photographs and say:

Now [Name of B], these photographs show people visiting exhibitions. [Name of A], you can look at them too. [Name of B], I'd like you to compare and contrast these photographs saying why you think people enjoy visiting exhibitions like these. Remember you have about a minute for this, so don't worry if I interrupt you.

Time Candidate B and say 'Thank you' after about a minute. Then say to Candidate A:

[Name of A] which of these two exhibitions would you like to visit?

Say 'Thank you' after Candidate A has been speaking for about twenty seconds.

Alternatively, they can be asked to discuss the example performances, saying which speaker they thought was more successful, and why. This can be followed with a feedback session in which the teacher makes sure that all the main points concerning effective or less successful interactions are covered. The next stage would involve focusing on the actual language used to manage the interaction. After a practice phase, the whole class might be asked to repeat the less successful task with a partner, incorporating the language presented and practised.

Example lesson – speaking in pairs and groups

The following lesson plan shows how these skills might be taught to an advanced group of learners.

Before class: The teacher finds a pre-recorded discussion in an appropriate coursebook.

In class: The teacher sets the scene and plays the recording. Students listen to the conversation and do a gist and/or specific information task, such as completing notes, true/false questions, multiple matching. They compare their answers in pairs and then listen again to check these. Students then receive a worksheet with a list of expressions, some of which are used in the conversation and some of which are not. They listen for a third time and tick the expressions they hear. Alternatively, students are given gapped sentences, with the expressions, for completion while they listen. Again, they compare answers in pairs, then check their answers in open class. To embed these expressions more strongly, students can be drilled in their use individually and in chorus.

Next, the teacher sets up a related group-work discussion task, monitors the groups as they conduct the discussion, and makes a note of which students are using the expressions. After drawing the discussions to a close, the teacher forms a new group made up of students who are using the expressions. This new group is given another related discussion topic. The rest of the class listen and keep a tally of the number of expressions they hear the group use. In the final feedback session, the teacher can comment on any errors heard while monitoring the groups (without being specific about who made the errors).

It is important that the gist or specific information listening task does not take up too much time. Its purpose is to focus attention on the conversation and it should be easy enough for students to complete the task successfully and then move on to the 'meat' of the lesson, i.e. the management of interaction expressions. As well as the expressions in the recording, more can be elicited from the class, and these can be noted. It is not a good idea, however, to teach too many expressions in one lesson. Students should be given an opportunity to construct variations on the expressions that have been presented, and should know that they are expected to use the expressions in their group discussion (and that they will be rewarded for doing so). The teacher might even offer a prize to the group who makes best use of the expressions.

Another approach could involve dividing the class into four groups. The members of each group work together, brainstorming points to make in the discussion. They appoint a representative to take part in the discussion – held between the four representatives of each group. The whole class listen to the discussion, monitoring their representative's performance. The representatives then go back to their group for advice on how they could perform better in the discussion. They then try the discussion task again, incorporating the advice they were given. In the feedback session, teachers do not single out individuals for criticism but do say whom they noticed using the expressions most effectively.

How to help students get to know the assessment criteria

It is a good idea for teachers to show learners the formal criteria that the assessor will be using in the exam, and give them hands-on experience of applying them to actual performances. Here are some ideas for activities that can be set up for this purpose:

video

objective
IELTS samples

- Students watch a video of an exam taking place, and assess the candidate's performance (some exam boards provide videos for teacher training purposes which can be shown to students).

- The teacher models a task, and students assess this performance.

✓✓
then

- Some students are chosen to act as candidates, and the teacher conducts a mock exam in front of the class. The other students assess each candidate's performance.

- Students do a practice exam in groups of three or four (as suggested in the sample lesson above). They then use the criteria to assess the performance of the person taking the 'candidate' role. This person can also assess himself or herself, and compare with the assessment given by the other students.

imp.

Any of these methods will help students to see that the assessor is not there just to record errors and complain about them to the interlocutor after they have left the room, but to 'draw' a complete picture of a candidate's performance, making sure that full credit is given for what was done well. It is important to make sure that when students assess one another they exercise sensitivity and remember to praise as well as criticise.

How to help students develop skills in managing interaction

Successful turn-taking involves knowing how to hesitate, how to indicate that you want to speak or to invite someone else to speak, how to express an opinion, agree or disagree, and so on. These functional aspects of the management of interaction need to be focused on in class.

An invaluable student resource for raising awareness of language that will help them to manage interaction in English is a set of function cards such as those used for indexing and cataloguing. Students can build up, keep, learn from, and add to their own reference-card file as they notice examples of the language in use. The idea can be introduced during a lesson as suggested below, and the set of cards can then be built up gradually during the course, one or two cards being introduced at a time.

 Function reference cards – Each student is provided (or provides themselves) with a set of record cards. The advantage of cards is that they are robust and easy to file in boxes or carry in pockets. Students are told that they are each going to make a set of reference cards to help them remember expressions that are useful when people are talking in a group. The teacher briefly explains the fact that we use language to do lots of things, for example, to *explain*, to *apologize*, to *interrupt*, to *agree* or *disagree* etc, and there are particular kinds of language used to express these uses, or **functions**, of language. To make this clear, the teacher chooses one function and writes it as a heading on the board. The students copy this as a heading (e.g. EXPRESSING MY OPINION) onto one of their cards, and suggest ways of giving an opinion. If they have a good idea, the teacher writes up the stem of the sentence, to make a list on the board, which the teacher

EXPRESSING MY OPINION
What I think is ...
It seems to me that ...
If you ask me ...
My view is ...
I really can't see why ...

can add to, if useful expressions have been missed. Students can be encouraged to produce more, or less formal, alternatives, and to think about when different expressions would be appropriate or inappropriate. The students copy the list onto their card, with notes on when each expression may be used.

The card resource can be put to a number of different uses, both in class and for self-study.

For example:
• Students should be encouraged to listen to as much English as possible, noticing examples of how people use language to do different things, and adding more expressions to their cards.
• Students can be recorded as they take part in speaking activities in pairs or groups. They can then listen to themselves and see if they can improve their turn-taking by using some of the expressions they have learned.
• Tapescripts in coursebooks can be used to analyse examples of native speaker interaction and look at the language used to manage turn-taking. This can also be done with recordings of radio or TV discussions, but it is then a far harder task!
• Students can review the language on their cards very easily, for example when travelling, or while waiting for other students to finish an activity.

How to help learners with interview tasks

Learners are likely to have had a lot of experience of talking about their personal circumstances, both in English and in other languages. They will be able to make some of their responses almost without thinking. It is for this reason that this task is so often used at the beginning of a test and is regarded as helping to make the candidates feel more relaxed.

Nevertheless, students need classroom practice in asking and responding to interview questions. Younger learners especially might not have thought about some of the things they are asked. They need to understand that the question is not being asked because the interlocutor really wants to know the answer, but so that she or he can hear them speak.

Another problem that may come up for adult learners is that even questions designed to be innocuous may provoke quite strong feelings. It is important for candidates to remember that they are not obliged to tell the truth in an interview task. Where mismatches occur between what they feel and what they can express, they should say what they can say, rather than struggling to express complex and disturbing emotions. The more opportunity students have had to ask and answer a wide variety of personal information questions, the better able they are to overcome these problems.

The kind of 'Find someone who ...' activity that many teachers use when getting to know new classes can easily be adapted to provide appropriate question and answer practice. In this activity, students are given a set of prompts (on cards – see right) which they must use to ask questions.

(handwritten margin note: 4 IELTS Part 1 (develop answers))

Teachers might try the following methods to generate ideas for prompt cards for such an activity:

Find someone who ...

has an unusual hobby
dislikes the same foods as you do
plans to study abroad next year
... and so on

- Adapting questions from exam scripts (available in exam handbooks) for interview tasks.
- Asking students to make up their own questions under topic headings (family, hobbies, future plans etc).
- Giving students sample answers and have them work out what the questions were.

If students devise the questions themselves, this also provides excellent practice in question formation.

With higher levels, it is important to practise giving extended responses to interview questions. Exam candidates are expected to be able to develop their answers beyond a simple one-, two-, or three-word response. A good way to begin is by raising awareness of how odd, unfriendly, or impolite very short responses sound. The first phase would involve using a pre-recorded sample or a transcript with a relatively unresponsive and a responsive candidate for students to compare. Alternately, the teacher can take the role of interviewee. Students can take it in turns to ask questions and the teacher can alternate between being responsive or unresponsive, perhaps in accordance with whether or not the question is well-formed or whether the questioner has used a new question form. Students then try their hands at producing an improved version of the exam task by providing extended responses.

In higher-level tests, where candidates are asked to interview each other, it is important that they show interest in each other's responses. This they can do by:

- making appropriate minimal responses (*mmm, aha, oh really?, I see* etc)
- using appropriate body language (smiling, nodding, eye contact, and leaning towards the other candidate)
- making sure that the next question builds on a previous response or question, as in the following example:

A: Do you have any **special plans** for the summer?

B: Well, I'm hoping to find a job and save enough money to go on holiday with a group of **friends**.

A: Where are you and your **friends** hoping to go?

B: We'd like to travel around Spain together. What about you, are you **planning** to go anywhere **special**?

Again, an awareness-raising approach works well. It is possible use some taped examples in which candidates show interest and others where they do not, or play the role of a candidate ourselves. In the weeks immediately before the exam, students can be asked to simulate this part of the test, taking it in turns to play the part of interlocutor and candidate(s).

It is important to point out to our students that no matter how familiar they might be with the interview task, they should never fall into the trap of memorizing and reproducing a speech or a set of responses in a fixed order. Questions can vary considerably from one examination session to another and interlocutors are often told to choose different sections of the script for each pair of candidates.

How to develop learners' discussion skills

The discussion task can be demanding for various reasons. Younger learners may never have considered the kinds of serious issues that are presented for discussion. Sometimes, although the topics are designed to be relatively uncontroversial, they can touch a raw nerve or occasionally even open up real conflict between candidates. More often, the discussion questions fail to strike a chord and candidates struggle to find an opinion to express.

It is vital to emphasize again that what the learners say during the test will not be 'taken down in evidence and used against them'. In most speaking tests, the examiners are not evaluating candidates' ability to think critically but their ability to express opinions, acknowledge and respond to opinions that others express, and develop a discussion collaboratively.

Regular class discussions help on many levels. By hearing a wide range of points of view, everyone can add to their store of opinions and come to feel more confident about their own views. Because they have such wide audiences, both exams and published exam materials often need to avoid sensitive issues such as drugs, race, sexuality, politics, and religion. Nevertheless, it is often these very issues that learners really want to talk about and, with sensitivity, they can often be aired in classroom discussions. Teachers are well-advised to check with those who have longer standing experience of a cultural context before introducing these topics if they themselves are new to the school, region, or country. In discussions like these, strong opinions very different from a student's own may be expressed, and valuable experience can be gained in contesting these views and defending a position. If we have a large class, we may not wish these discussions to be teacher-led (although teachers will probably want to monitor the tone of the discussions, as well as their language content). In this case, students can carry out their discussion in groups and appoint a spokesperson to report back to the rest of the class. The vital thing is that everyone gets to hear many different points of view.

A good way of helping learners generate opinions, or of allowing them to express opinions that they might not feel safe 'owning', is through traditional debates. Students can work in groups helping the main debaters prepare to argue their case. In this way, everyone takes part and has a stake in the outcome of the debate. The class can then vote on the motion or invite another class as audience and ask them to vote. A less formal approach involves students speaking 'for' someone they know well. They say what they imagine their grandfather, or a favourite celebrity, or girlfriend would say about an issue.

The management of interaction skills, discussed above in relation to the other tasks, is just as crucial here and the same approach works well. In addition, televised and broadcast debates and talkback shows are a good source of the kind of language that learners will need.

How to prepare students for sustained (one-way) speaking tasks

Although most people are quite capable of keeping up a monologue for a minute or more when they have something they really want to say, it is not so easy to sustain a long turn in a classroom or exam setting when the topic is set by someone else. Students need regular practice to build up their confidence that they can manage this kind of speaking. Short activities, like those described below, can be used regularly throughout the exam preparation to help them to do this. As they gain confidence, the speaking time can be extended to two, three, or even five minutes; and the listener can take on the more formal role of examiner, evaluating their partner's performance in terms of the exam criteria (as with some activities described earlier in this chapter). An additional skill that students can also learn in connection with this activity is how, by **listening with full attention**, they can help the person speaking to feel comfortable and continue speaking without losing their way. Listening with full attention involves:

- looking towards the speaker
- showing interest by facial expressions and gestures: nodding, smiling, frowning etc, as appropriate
- using 'back-channelling' techniques. These are short verbal expressions that do not interrupt but simply show that you are listening, such as: *I see ... yes ... mmm ... did you? ... uh-huh ...*
- 'echoing' what the speaker says, to encourage them to say more. For example:

> **Speaker:** *... and I've never been back to that place since we went that time ...*
>
> **Listener:** *... you've never been back ...*
>
> **Speaker:** *... no, and it's a shame because I shall never forget that holiday.*

Here are various tasks and games that can be used to give students practice and confidence with sustained speaking:

 Sustained speaking and attentive listening – for this activity, the students work in pairs. The teacher writes a topic on the board and each student must in turn speak about this topic for one minute, timed by the teacher. While one student is speaking, the other must listen without interrupting. When the speaker finishes, and the teacher has given the word, the listener may ask them two questions about what they have said. When the activity has finished, the students discuss for one minute in their pairs what made it easy or difficult, and this can be followed by a brief class discussion and some action points for next time.

 Just a minute – another way of building confidence is to turn the speaking task into a game. The popular UK radio programme, *Just a Minute*, provides a ready-made framework. In this game, contestants must try to speak on a given topic for one minute without hesitating for more than a few seconds or repeating the same phrase. The other contestants can challenge the speaker if they believe there has been either hesitation or repetition. If the referee supports the challenge, the successful challenger takes up where the other speaker left off. Whoever is still speaking when the minute is up, wins a point. This game can be easily adapted to the classroom context, with teams competing against each other. Students should appreciate that speaking for a minute without undue hesitation or repetition is very like what they will be expected to do in the exam.

 Describe and draw – in this light-hearted exercise, one student describes a picture to a partner, who attempts to draw it. Using bizarre or quirky illustrations makes this more fun, as does prohibiting the use of the name of the object shown.

 Describe and identify – this works better with older learners, who can sometimes be self-conscious about their artistic ability (or lack of it). In this case, each student has a set of similar illustrations, usually arranged in a different order. One student describes two or three of these while the other listens and tries to work out which illustrations have been described.

Like 'Just a minute', these last two activities are actually very close to the tasks used in tests where candidates are examined in pairs. Learners should realize that their listening skills are also tested in most speaking exams. In the exam, candidates may take it in turns to present information, but the candidate who is listening is often asked a question by the interlocutor at the end of their partner's presentation. This might involve saying, for example, which of a group of pictures the speaker did or did not talk about.

How to help students talk about pictures

Pictures are commonly used as prompts in speaking exams. Students need to be reassured that it is not their general knowledge that is being tested. No examiner expects candidates to identify the exact location or the people illustrated, so they should not let themselves be put off if there is something they do not recognize. In fact, being able to express oneself tentatively through the use of modal verbs of possibility (*may, might,* and *could*) and deduction (*must* and *can't*) as well as adverbs such as *perhaps, maybe, possibly,* and *probably* is something that is tested in this version of the presentation task. A candidate who can say, *The photograph might have been taken somewhere in the south of France but I'm not really sure. Perhaps it's a seaside town in Italy or some other country.* will be rewarded for their command of English, even if the examiner knows it is actually a picture of the west coast of Ireland.

Another way to build confidence is to make sure candidates are aware that although vocabulary is usually tested as a component of range, the presentation task is not solely a vocabulary test. If they do not know the word for something that appears in a photograph or they can't remember a term they want to use in a topic presentation, it is far better to use communication strategies such as circumlocution (*She's holding a … a thing that's used for getting corks out of bottles.*), than to freeze and say, *I don't know how to say that.*

How to provide pronunciation practice within an exam course

Pronunciation may be handled on an exam course through a combination of short classroom activities designed to raise awareness of features which are of general importance, and worksheets for individual study and practice using a language laboratory or other auditory support. If the teacher is able to spend time on individual tutorials, these offer opportunities for raising students' awareness of their particular pronunciation difficulties and the need to work on them. The following ideas for short (10–15 minutes) classroom activities can be adapted for use by individuals or groups.

Here are some ideas to help students work on their awareness and pronunciation of **individual sounds**:

 The teacher puts together a set of word pairs which rhyme but whose endings are spelt differently. The words are spread randomly across a sheet of paper and a copy given to each student. The challenge is for them to identify the pairs which rhyme.

 On a piece of paper are written ten sentences, each of which contains several instances of the same sound. Each student gets a copy and is asked to identify how many times the same sound occurs in a sentence.

 The teacher identifies five sounds which cause particular difficulty for individual students (or asks the students to suggest sounds which they have problems with). For homework, each student prepares five sentences including as many instances as possible of the sounds they have difficulty with. Having done this, the students read their sentences aloud to the teacher, for checking purposes. Then they are put in pairs and asked to dictate their sentences to each other. This forces the students to speak clearly and concentrate on pronouncing every word correctly.

 A native speaker (perhaps the teacher or a colleague) records a spoken text in which they make a number of deliberate pronunciation mistakes. The students are given a script of what was said, as if there were no mistakes. When the tape is played to the students, they must identify the pronunciation mistakes.

Here are some ways in which students can improve their appreciation of **stress** in pronunciation:

 The teacher puts together a set of words and/or short utterances which have different stress patterns. These are written randomly across a sheet of paper and a copy made for each student. They are then asked to group the utterances according to their stress patterns.

 Students are given a list of sentences containing words which are used as both nouns and verbs. They must decide whether the pronunciation is the same in both cases, or whether the stress changes, depending on whether they are being used as nouns or verbs. Students may need dictionaries to do this. They then practise reading the sentences aloud.

 The teacher generates a very simple and obvious dialogue between two people, and writes this script as a pattern of stresses, with just a few words included to guide the students towards a solution. A copy of the script is given to each pair of students and they are asked to work together to think of words and utterances which might fill the gaps, and which fit the stress patterns indicated.

 The same sentence is written several times on a piece of paper, with the stress on different words in the sentence. Students practise saying the sentence in these different ways, and discuss how the stress movement changes the meaning of the utterance.

Intonation is another important aspect of pronunciation that can be addressed with short classroom activities:

 The teacher thinks of an utterance which can be said in a number of different ways, giving it a wide variety of meanings depending on the speaker's intention. The utterance is written on the board. The students come up to the front in turn, and the teacher whispers to them the emotion they are to express when saying the sentence aloud. The student performs, and the class has to guess what the emotion was.

 The teacher finds, or makes, a tape recording of people saying things with different sorts of emotional force. Students are asked to deduce the emotion behind each utterance. They then discuss how the shape of the intonation pattern works to create this impression.

 Thinking of a well-known utterance which can be said with a reasonably dramatic intonation, the teacher voices it in front of the class without opening his or her mouth. This way, the students hear the pitch movement, but no words. They guess what it is that the teacher is saying.

Conclusions   In this chapter we have
- considered the different formats that speaking exams can take.
- described four widely-used types of exam task: interview (question and answer), presentation (individual long turn), collaborative negotiation task, and discussion.
- discussed the roles of the various participants in speaking exams – assessor, interlocutor, candidate(s).
- analysed the sub-skills of speaking, such as discourse management, interactive communication, grammatical and lexical resource use, and pronunciation, and looked at how these are tested and assessed.
- discussed some of the problems that students have in developing these different skills and suggested activities that might help.
- emphasized the need for students to be well-informed about the exam format and procedures, and given ideas for simulating these in class, using authentic materials such as interlocutor scripts and formal assessment criteria.
- explored ideas for preparing students who will be examined in pairs.
- commented on the different demands made on students taking exams at lower and higher levels, as reflected in task formats, content and assessment criteria.

8 How to teach for low-level exams

What is different about low-level exams?

Low-level reading and writing

- **Reading for general understanding**
- **Reading to test knowledge of how the language works**
- **Directed and free writing**
- **Low-level listening**
- **Low-level speaking**
- **Low-level grammar and vocabulary**

What is different about low-level exams?

Most of the teaching ideas and examples in this book so far have been based on exams at intermediate level (CEF level B2 / ALTE level 3) and above. At these levels, students need special training to prepare them for specific exam tasks, but this is less likely to be true for exams at lower levels. Preparation for low-level exams is more easily integrated into a general English course, since the exams are shorter and test a more limited range of skills and knowledge. The grammar, vocabulary, topic areas, and language functions tested are practised in general elementary and pre-intermediate coursebooks, so little specific exam preparation is needed. This makes it easy to accommodate within the same class students who are preparing to take an exam and those who are not.

It is sometimes argued that there is little point in learners taking exams until their English is at a level where they can enter for an exam which has demonstrable value in terms of what they can do with it (for example, get a job, study abroad). However, lower-level exams exist to fulfil certain aims:

- to provide a measure of progress from one level of ability to another
- to increase motivation and challenge for those students who work best towards clear goals and objectives
- to provide information to the students themselves, as well as to their parents, sponsors, employers etc. about their competence in English in relation to external requirements
- to familiarize learners with preparing for and taking exams, and to prepare them for the more demanding challenges of higher-level exams
- to provide points of achievement along the journey of learning

Low-level reading and writing

In lower-level exams, reading and writing are often tested together on a single paper. This makes sense, since reading and writing are closely connected in the real world, and writers often glean ideas for their own writing from things that they have read elsewhere. Reading and writing work together and support each other in low-level language learning and exams. For example, the text of a letter set for reading comprehension in the Reading section of the exam may also prove useful as a model for a letter-writing task in the Writing section. Many writing tasks involve careful reading, not just of the question but also of other input material which is to be used in the answer. A good reader who writes poorly may lose marks through using incorrect spelling or grammar to write the answers to reading questions, while a good writer who reads poorly may lose marks, however good their writing, if they have not read the question carefully enough.

The kinds of texts that candidates are required to read or write, even at the lowest level of proficiency, are the kind that they would meet in real world contexts where English is used. Although most texts are specially written or adapted for the exam, every effort is made to make them look and sound as authentic as possible. The following list gives an idea of how many different kinds of text we need to be able to read and/or write in order to cope, even at a basic level, in a new language:

- signs, notices, labels, and simple instructions
- advertisements, guides, brochures etc.
- simple maps and street plans
- timetables
- short informative articles
- book or film reviews, letters, messages, emails, faxes etc.
- forms and questionnaires

Although examples of such texts can be found in coursebooks, it is a good idea for teachers to make their own collection of authentic texts, of the types listed above, to use in exam preparation lessons. Learners enjoy handling authentic material and such a collection has many uses. Learners can also be encouraged to notice the English used in signs, advertisements, songs, film reviews etc, and to make their own collection of words and expressions to bring and share with their classmates. The use of English is so widespread that examples are easy to find, and not only in English-speaking countries. Making the connection between the reading and writing tasks they practise for their exam, and the ways they see English being used in real life, will help to equip students with the skills they need to process written language.

Exam candidates are required to demonstrate a range of reading and writing skills, which are tested through a variety of task types. Teachers need to develop a clear understanding of the different task types, in order to prepare their students as effectively as possible. The following sections of this chapter deal separately with reading tasks and writing tasks, although these are often combined at low levels into a single exam paper.

Reading for general understanding

In communicative approaches to reading, a key principle is: 'simplify the task, not the text' – as long as the task is set at an appropriate level of difficulty, learners should be able to make sense of most common kinds of text. The ability to 'make sense' is a vital skill for low-level learners coping in real English language environments, where they will encounter input language which is well above the level of what they can produce themselves. Most reading tasks are therefore designed to encourage reading for general understanding and important information, as the following example test question shows.

The candidate looks at a set of pictures of public signs or notices. There is one multiple choice or matching question for each picture.

- Look at the text in each question.
- What does it say?
- Mark the letter next to the correct explanation – A, B, or C – on your answer sheet.

Example:

NEVER LEAVE LUGGAGE UNATTENDED

A You must stay with your luggage at all times.

B Do not let someone else look after your luggage.

C Remember your luggage when you leave.

From *PET Specifications* (University of Cambridge Local Examinations Syndicate)

The task here is to understand the gist of each notice, the sort of context where it would appear, and who is supposed to read it. Misunderstandings tend to occur when a student focuses on isolated words rather than on the message as a whole. For example, focusing on the words 'never leave' or 'luggage unattended' in the notice above does not help the student to choose between A, B, and C; they need to recognize the meaning of the whole phrase in order to select A as the correct answer.

Although signs and notices like these are very common in English language environments, they are rarely introduced into published materials for teaching and learning English, and students who attempt these tasks without preparation often find them difficult. Yet relatively little practice is necessary to teach students to match form with meaning, because the language found on signs and notices is quite formulaic, and the same words and phrases appear again and again, always with the same meaning:

Keep ... (off the grass / out / left / in a cool place / etc)
Do not ... (disturb / touch / walk on the grass / etc)
No ... (parking / smoking / cycling / etc)
Special ... (offer / event / request / etc)
(Seats / Rooms / Photocopying facilities) ... **available**
(Staff / Adults / Residents) ... **only**
(Mobile phones / Dogs / Breakages) ... **must be** ... (switched off / carried / paid for)

Understanding signs and notices – for this ten-minute activity, the teacher draws a square on the board to represent a notice, and writes something inside the square (for example, 'Rooms should be vacated by 12 noon'). The students are asked where they would expect to see this notice; one student explains what it means, doing this as if explaining the notice to a friend. The class then moves on to consider two or three other situations where we might find notices of a similar kind. For example:

1 The doctor's surgery has a notice telling patients to collect their prescriptions from the reception.
2 The supermarket has a notice telling customers to return their trolleys to the trolley-park when they have finished their shopping.
3 A jar of jam has a label on it telling consumers not to eat it after the expiry date.

The words of each notice are elicited from the students, and written on the board. In these examples, we would expect:

1 Prescriptions should be collected from reception.
2 Trolleys should be returned to the trolley-park after shopping.
3 This jam should not be eaten after the expiry date.

Later, as students start to bring in their own examples of signs and notices that they have found, they can take over the teacher's role in this activity.

 Making sense of a longer text – in this activity, the candidate reads a number of statements, and has to decide whether they are right or wrong, correct or incorrect, according to the information given in the text. There is also a third option, which is that the information is not given in the text. [An example is given on page 125.]

It can be difficult to persuade students that they do not need to read every word of the text in order to understand well enough to do the task, and to wean them away from their dictionaries. This is why it is so important to practise reading in class, and take learners step by step through strategies which, if practised regularly, give them the best chance of developing into fluent, fast readers who are not held up by unfamiliar words or redundant information. To make sense of a piece of reading material, it can be counter-productive to pay too much attention to detail. Two approaches to understanding longer texts are suggested:

 Having chosen a text with accompanying questions (multiple choice, true/false, open questions etc), the teacher writes the title of the text on the board. Students say what they already know – or expect to find

Read the article about shopping in Britain.
Are sentences 21–27 'Right' (A) or 'Wrong' (B)?

If there is not enough information to answer 'Right' (A) or 'Wrong' (B), choose 'Doesn't say' (C).

For questions 21–27, mark **A, B** or **C** on your answer sheet.

SHOPPING HOURS in BRITAIN

Shopping hours in Britain are changing. Until a few years ago, shops opened at nine o'clock in the morning and closed at half past five or six o'clock in the evening. Some also closed for an hour for lunch. In many towns, shops were closed on Wednesday afternoons. On Sundays, nothing was open. But now some shops are open longer hours. Some big shops and many supermarkets never close! If you need a litre of milk or some bread at midnight, you can easily buy it.

For people who work long hours or people who often work at night or early in the morning, like doctors, the new shopping hours are good. If someone finishes work at five o'clock in the morning, they can go to the supermarket on their way home and buy some breakfast or a newspaper or anything else they may need.

But not everyone thinks the new shopping hours are a good thing. Some people say that Sunday is a holiday – who wants to work in a supermarket on a Sunday? But shops are very busy at the weekend and longer shopping hours are here to stay.

---

21 In the past, some shops closed at lunchtime.

   A Right   **B** Wrong   **C** Doesn't say

22 A few years ago, shops also closed on Saturday afternoons.

   A Right   **B** Wrong   **C** Doesn't say

23 Today, all shops are open for longer hours.

   A Right   **B** Wrong   **C** Doesn't say

etc.

Adapted from *KET Practice Tests Plus* by Peter Lucantoni (Longman)

out – in that text, on the basis of its title. They will even be able to predict some of the vocabulary. Then the teacher gives out the text and questions, but asks the students to cover the text and only look at the questions. Students read through the questions, making sure that they understand each one, and predict what the answers might be. They can compare answers in pairs. Then they look at the text and compare their answers with the information given there. Finally, the teacher checks that the students have understood the answers given in the text and comments on useful language found there.

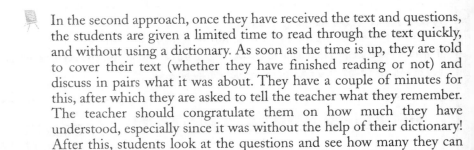

In the second approach, once they have received the text and questions, the students are given a limited time to read through the text quickly, and without using a dictionary. As soon as the time is up, they are told to cover their text (whether they have finished reading or not) and discuss in pairs what it was about. They have a couple of minutes for this, after which they are asked to tell the teacher what they remember. The teacher should congratulate them on how much they have understood, especially since it was without the help of their dictionary! After this, students look at the questions and see how many they can answer before reading the text again. Having done this, they then scan the text to check their answers, and to find any information that they could not remember from their first reading. Finally, the teacher checks the answers and comments on the language used in the text.

As well as using published materials, teachers can find their own texts and write exam-type questions to accompany them. Short extracts of authentic text from books, magazines, or the Internet can be used. The more students practise reading for general understanding, the more fluent and confident they will become. This will help them not only in their reading but also when they come to write in English.

Exam questions and coursebook exercises can readily be adapted to give students practice in quickly getting the sense of a piece of text, as shown here.

Example lesson

This is a **multiple-matching task** which involves matching different pieces of information. In this activity, three people and five websites are described. The task is to decide which of the websites would be most useful for each person. [See page 127.]

The main difficulty with this kind of multiple-matching task is that there is not a simple one-to-one correspondence between people and (in this case) websites. The task is complicated by the fact that there are more websites than people, and it is important for students to keep an open mind as they sort through the various pieces of information in front of them. If students are getting the answers wrong, it is probably that they were misled by certain key words which seemed to fit the description. They need to be reminded that it is important to check that *all* the details match up, and that there is only one completely correct match. If they decide too quickly, they may well miss a clue and make the wrong choice. In this example, the correct matches are: Lisa and 'Our World' (where she can chat with other young people about clothes and music), Ken and 'Music Matters' (which is a specialist music website offering all the advice he needs on what to buy and where to buy, and on prices), Oscar and 'Connections' (which has information about both travel and careers, and lots of news and advice from around the world to help him decide where to go).

Given a task of the type described above, students can start by looking at the information given about each of the people, and marking the key points.

Recommended websites

1 Marketplace

This is an amazing list of stores, both High Street and on-line, regularly updated. Compare prices to find the cheapest goods, read reviews of goods tested by experts or send in your own users' report. Whether you're looking for clothes, CDs, DVDs, televisions or holidays, you'll find them here.

2 Lifelines

Lifelines is probably one of the biggest sites on the web. It covers a huge range of subjects from package holidays to job opportunities, designer clothes to world sports results and links you to sites which have paid to join their list. Especially strong on family and home ideas.

3 Connections

Connections is a fashionable site covering all essential things – news, sports results, advice and articles from all over the world – as well as providing serious information about planning your career and generally organizing your life. Lots of links to other sites for ideas about working abroad, safe travel, etc.

4 Music Matters

Plenty of news and concert reviews here. You also have the opportunity to meet and chat with other fans of your favourite bands. And the Music Matters on-line store is full of all types of music. Buy tickets for all the best bands and festivals – there are sometimes special prices. You can also check out the top 40 pop songs.

5 Our World

A site for young people to meet and discuss what interests them – fashion, pop culture, music, problems, careers. Post your questions on the site's noticeboard and you'll soon get lots of replies. There's also advice from professionals, so if you want to ask about health, money or education you can get some serious answers.

Lisa enjoys visiting sites aimed at people of her own age. She loves chatting on the Internet and finding out what other people think about her main interests, which are clothes and music.

Ken is building a music library of his favourite bands and classical works. He likes using the internet for advice on what to buy, the best price and where to buy it.

Oscar wants to keep up to date with world affairs. He's planning to travel when he leaves university and wants advice about opportunities overseas and career possibilities when he returns.

Adapted from
PET Masterclass – Student Book
by Annette Capel & Rosemary Nixon
(Oxford University Press)

They can be asked to predict what sort of website would suit each person. They are then told to read through the website descriptions and mark any which appear to match the first person. More than one apparently suitable match may be found at this point. They go on to do the same for the second person, and continue down through the list until they have matched a website to each of them. Students can then compare their answers in pairs, and discuss what helped them to decide which websites made the best matches.

In contrast to the kinds of tasks described above, which test general understanding and the ability to select specific information, other reading tasks focus on the use of particular features of language in a text. They test candidates' knowledge of how words and sentences fit together or share certain aspects of meaning. For example, in the following CEF level A2 (ALTE level 1) task, the candidate must understand how the connectors *and*, *but*, *so*, and *because* are used in order to chose correctly from the answers (A–I) to fill the gaps in the email. To make the task more difficult, there are eight possible answers but only six gaps.

```
Hi Jimi
I'm in hospital with a broken leg! It was
my birthday last week (1) ................. . Yesterday
we had some free time (2) ................. with our
skateboards. In our town you can either
skate by the river (3) ................. . The park is
better than the river (4) ................. . Rashid
skated down the hill first (5) ................. . I
had no problem with the hill (6) ................. at
the bottom. And now I'm in hospital with a
broken leg!
Nick.
```

A or in the park
B and I loved it
C but I couldn't stop
D so we decided to go out
E because I fell over
F and then I followed him
G and Rashid gave me a new skateboard
H but he was second
I because it has got a steep hill

From a City and Guilds Pitman International ESOL sample paper at Access Level

Published material can be easily adapted to provide convenient texts for use in classroom activities that help learners to understand how the language works and develop their ability to cope with tasks like this one.

 Recognizing patterns in text – the teacher prepares (or finds in a book) a text such as the one above, underlines each connector and removes the piece of information following it. Using the example above, the text would look like this:

> Hi Jimi
> I'm in hospital with a broken leg! It was my birthday
> last week <u>and</u> .... Yesterday we had some free time <u>so</u>
> .... with our skateboards. In our town you can either
> skate by the river <u>or</u> .... The park is better than
> the river <u>because</u> .... Rashid skated down the hill
> first <u>and</u> .... I had no problem with the hill <u>but</u>
> .... at the bottom. And now I'm in hospital with a
> broken leg!
> Nick.

Students work in pairs to predict what the missing information might be. They will come up with a range of different texts, which can then be read aloud so that the rest of the class can hear and discuss them. After this, the teacher gives out the missing sections of text from the original version, but in the wrong order. The students are given time to fit them into the appropriate spaces, and discuss any similarities and differences between this 'model' text and the one they wrote themselves. Finally, the class can discuss which of all the texts produced (including the original one) was the most interesting!

Directed and free writing

Just as most reading tasks involve an element of writing, so most writing tasks involve an element of reading. This section takes a look at two types of low-level writing task: directed writing and free writing.

Directed writing

The sorts of directed writing tasks set at low CEF/ALTE levels include simple form-filling, gapped texts, and correcting errors in spelling and punctuation. An example is given below of each of these.

The simplest **form-filling** task, here illustrated at CEF level A1 (ALTE Breakthrough level), involves giving basic personal information (which need not be 'true' as long as it is correctly presented – it is quite acceptable to invent the information!).

Sports Club Form

Family *Name*: ....

Telephone Number: ....

Sex: ....

Age: ....

Favourite Sport: ....

From a City and Guilds Pitman International ESOL Sample Paper at Preliminary Level

---

Candidates must not only understand the headings given on the form, but must also give the required information in the correct form. The use of block capitals for name and nationality, and the correct way of writing telephone numbers and dates of birth, can be modelled on the classroom board before the students are given their own copy of the form to complete. The complexity of the form-filling activity, and the amount of information required, increases gradually through CEF levels A2 and B1 (ALTE levels 1 and 2).

129

A form-filling activity can be extended by pairing students and getting them to interview each other, perhaps as a role-play between immigration official and overseas visitor, or between hotel receptionist and guest. Having first practised the questions, the interviewer asks the interviewee for the information needed to complete the form. Spelling aloud, and correct pronunciation of numbers and dates, can also be practised.

In **gap-fill** tasks, because only single words, numbers, and occasional short phrases are tested, candidates are expected to spell correctly and incorrect spelling is penalized. Here is a level 1 task, showing the text of a postcard which must be completed by writing one word in each space.

Dear Alvaro,

I'm having a great (0) .... here in Spain!
The weather (41) .... very good. It has (42) .... very
hot every day and (43) .... hasn't rained.

This morning, we (44) .... to the beach for a swim.
Tomorrow we (45) .... going shopping in the afternoon.
I want to buy (46) .... presents to (47) .... home
for my family. There's also a big castle (48) .... a hill
that I want to visit.

I arrive at (49) .... airport at 11.30 on Monday night.
I will phone (50) .... on Tuesday morning and tell you
about my holiday.

See you soon!

Pietro

From *KET Practice Tests Plus*
by Peter Lucantoni (Longman)

Students need to learn that they must read the whole sentence in order to ensure that the word they write is correct, and that it is written in the correct form. A student who writes *be* in the sentence 'It has ____ very hot every day' will not get any marks, even though they have recognized that the verb *be* must be used in the space. Sometimes there may be more than one correct answer; for example, in the text above, the answer to number (44) could be *went, walked, drove, cycled* etc. As long as the sentence makes sense and the correct form of the word is used, the student will get the mark.

A variation on this task that would make a useful classroom activity would be to choose a text and make two versions of it, taking out different words in each text. For example, the teacher could make a second version of the above text which looks like this:

Dear Alvaro,

I'm having a great (**Example**: <u>time</u>) here in Spain! The weather is very good. It (1)_____ been very hot (2)_____ day and it hasn't rained. This morning we went to (3)_____ beach for a swim. Tomorrow we are (4)_____ shopping in the afternoon. I want to (5)_____ some presents to take home for (6)_____ family. There's also a big castle on a hill that I want (7)_____ visit.

I arrive at the airport (8)_____ 11.30 on Monday night. I (9)_____ phone you on Tuesday morning and tell (10)_____ about my holiday.

See you soon!

Pietro

With the students divided into two groups, A and B, a copy of one text is given to every student in Group A, and a copy of the other text to all in Group B. Each student has to fill in the missing words in their text. The students in Group A then find a partner in Group B and compare their texts, remembering to check for correct spelling. Finally, everyone is shown the complete text and reads it aloud in chorus.

Free writing

Without the constraints of having to fit their words to a prepared text, free-writing tasks allow the candidate to show what they are capable of when starting with a blank piece of paper. Naturally, candidates are not expected to be able to write faultless English, and the main emphasis of assessment is on the success of the communication. The task is usually to write a short essay, letter, or message. There may be a required number of words (minimum and maximum), or a space may be provided on the paper to indicate the length of answer required. Students need to learn to read the instructions carefully so that they know what is required. This *Access* level writing task must be completed in just 20 to 40 words:

Writing Part 3
You want to book a holiday. Write a letter to a travel agent.

- *Say where*
- *Say how long for*
- *Find out the cost*

Do not write an address. Write 20-40 words.

From a City and Guilds Pitman International ESOL Sample Paper at Access Level

A candidate who includes the three required pieces of information, and formulates the piece of writing appropriately, will be considered to have completed the task successfully even if there are mistakes in spelling and use of language. Students therefore need to learn the correct layout of notices, postcards, faxes, personal letters etc. as well as the basic conventions of language use in these different genres. The teacher's own collection of authentic texts is invaluable here, although we can also find model texts in the reading and listening sections of exam papers. These can be used to show students what a note, postcard, letter, or fax looks like and how it should be laid out on the page.

You would like to study in Australia. Your family have given you the address of some old friends you have never met.

Task One

Write a letter to the Australian family to:

- introduce yourself and give them some news of your own family
- say why you want to go to Australia
- ask if you can stay with them
- ask about language schools near the Australian family

From *CELS Handbook* (University of Cambridge Local Examinations Syndicate)

This is a level 2 task, where candidates are expected to write around 100–150 words. Such a task is most often a letter. Separate marks are usually awarded for 'task completion' and for 'language'. In the above example, 'task completion' would mean that the piece of writing produced is clearly a letter (that is, it begins with 'Dear …' and ends with an appropriate salutation, such as 'Yours sincerely' or 'Best wishes'). In addition, it includes all the information required in the task rubric, and organizes this information in such a way that the reader has no difficulty in following it. 'Language' is assessed separately, and it is the student's general control and range of language which is assessed, not the number of individual mistakes made. Again, the impression made on the reader is central to the assessment. If the student comes across as a confident user of the language at their level, demonstrating generally good control and an ambitious range of structures and vocabulary, the mark awarded for language will be high. Frequent and erratic errors and poor punctuation, which have a negative effect on the reader, lead to a low mark for language. 'Task completion' and 'language' are equally important.

Students can best prepare for these free-writing activities through regular practice. Tasks can be set for homework, marked for task and language according to criteria published by the exam boards, and discussed in class. When marking, it is important not to focus too much on errors. Creativity and ambition are rewarded in the exam, so praise should be given for attempts which show that the student is stretching their knowledge, rather than simply playing safe and using correct but basic formulas.

Low-level listening

The aim of reading and writing exams at low levels is to test candidates' ability to carry out simple but authentic tasks in English. This is also true for listening and speaking exams. Learners are expected to be able to make some sense of real spoken English, and to be able to communicate some sort of conversational response, from the very beginning of their studies. In listening, the task might be to recognize the correct conversational response, as in the level 2 examples shown below. This kind of task requires familiarity with 'real' spoken English and a good sense of what is appropriate and polite. Sensitivity to what 'sounds right' is developed through repeated exposure to authentic spoken English, so if students have access to TV and videos they should be encouraged to watch programmes with plenty of good dialogue. Even if they don't understand much of what they hear, they will be training their ear to the sound patterns of English, and picking up a sense of appropriate responses.

In this example, the first part of the exchange is heard by the candidate and they must decide which of the four responses is correct.

---

1 'Hi! Great to see you after so long.'
   A. Hello. Nice to see you too.
   B. Not much really.
   C. What're you going to do?
   D. See you soon.

2 'Fancy going to the cinema tonight?'
   A. Why can't you?
   B. Isn't there?
   C. Not really.
   D. No I'm not.

3 'I am sorry I'm late.'
   A. That's right.
   B. Of course not.
   C. Don't worry.
   D. You're welcome.

From a City and Guilds Pitman International ESOL sample paper at Achiever Level

---

Listening tests require candidates to pick out important and relevant information from recordings of speech which, while specially scripted, are nevertheless as close to real-life dialogue or monologue as possible. They may even be adapted from authentic speech, for example, recordings of radio programmes or automatic answering machines. The kinds of text types which feature in many exams include:

- announcements at railway stations and airports
- traffic information given on the radio
- public announcements made at sporting events or pop concerts
- instructions given by police or customs officials

Listening for gist

When we listen to real speech, even in our own mother tongue, we do not pick up every word yet we still manage, if we are concentrating sufficiently, to understand and focus on what is really important or interesting. Language learners need to develop this skill of 'tuning in' to what is really essential right from the start, and the kinds of tasks set in listening exams are designed to encourage this.

In listening tests, there is always a pause to allow candidates to look at the question before they hear the recording. Students need to learn that they should use this time to think of what the answer might be, so that they know what they are listening for. If they listen with a purpose, they are less likely to be confused or distracted by redundant material which they do not need to pay attention to.

This sample listening task consists of a series of short, recorded, spoken texts with a single multiple choice question on each. The options are presented as pictures. A typical question is shown here:

3 What are Kevin and Sally going to do tonight?

A ☐    B ☐   C ☐   D ☐

K: *What shall we do tonight? It's a bit cold to go out.*
S: *There's a good film on TV ... or we could have a game of cards. Or I'm quite happy just reading.*
K: *Let's watch the film. I've got nothing to read, and I always lose at cards.*

Adapted from *PET Gold Exam Maximiser* by Jacky Newbrook & Judith Wilson (Longman)

 Listening for gist (short dialogues) – material such as this may be used to give learners practice at getting the gist of what they are listening to. Having played the dialogue once, the teacher asks the students how many speakers there are, where they are, and what they are talking about. The students are also told that they have to answer one question about the dialogue, and asked to guess what the question is going to be. If they do this easily, they can be asked what they think the correct answer is, and also what other, 'wrong' answers there might be. Finally, students are shown the question as it is presented in the exam.

Another kind of listening task is a longer text with several multiple choice or true/false questions. It is more difficult because candidates have to think about more than one question while they are listening. [See page 135.]

This example shows very clearly just how much redundant information is included in the text, and why it is really important for students to prepare carefully by looking at the questions, so that they know which cues to listen out for. There is always quite a long lead-in to the first important piece of information, as in the example opposite where Jenny says what the age range for the computer game is; this gives the students time to get used to the speakers' voices and the topic of their conversation. Notice also how there is a lot of information, that is irrelevant for the test, between the street (Marsden street) where the shop is and the number of the shop (29).

Listen to Jenny talking to Mark about buying a computer game.

For questions 11 – 15, tick ☑ A, B or C.
You will hear the conversation twice.

Adapted from *KET Handbook* (University of Cambridge Local Examinations Syndicate)

EXAMPLE

0	The name of the computer game is	A	City 2010	☑
		B	City 2001	☐
		C	City 2100	☐

11	The game is **not** good for people under	A	eight.	☐
		B	ten.	☐
		C	twelve.	☐

12	Black's PC shop is in	A	Cambridge.	☐
		B	London.	☐
		C	Peterstown.	☐

13	The address of the shop is	A	29 Hunter Road.	☐
		B	29 Walker Street.	☐
		C	29 Marsden Street.	☐

14	The last day you can get a free game is	A	Monday.	☐
		B	Thursday.	☐
		C	Friday.	☐

15	The computer game cost	A	£26.	☐
		B	£30.	☐
		C	£48.	☐

Audioscript

F	Hi, Mark. What are you doing?
M	Hello, Jenny. Shopping for a present for my little brother.
F	I bought *my* brother a computer game called City two thousand and ten. He plays with it for hours.
M	How old is he?
F	10.
M	*(Disappointed)* Oh - my brother's twelve.
F	That's OK. This game's good for eight to thirteen year olds.
M	Great! Where did you buy it?
F	In Black's PC shop. I looked everywhere in Cambridge and Peterstown, but I had to go to a shop in London to find it.
M	Where is the shop?
F	In Marsden street. You know Hunter Road? Turn left at the end and it's opposite Walker's department store at number twenty nine.
M	I can go there next Thursday.
F	That's good. Next week from Monday to Friday you get a second game free!
M	Great. How much was your brother's game?
F	*(thinking)* I bought two games that day and paid forty-eight pounds altogether, so my brother's game was twenty six pounds.
M	Oh, less than thirty! That's not bad. Thanks, Jenny.

If we find that our students are having problems with longer texts, a good strategy is to give them copies of the tapescript after the second listening, and ask them to double-check their choices before telling them what the right answers are. It may also be helpful to get them to mark on the tapescript where a section relating to a particular question begins and ends. This will alert them to important parts of the conversation that they have overlooked, and show them that just because a detail seems to fit, it is not automatically the right answer.

Listening for specific information

Some listening tasks require the candidate to listen for very specific pieces of information. Here is an example task that involves listening to a recorded message. The information which the candidate is expected to fill in consists

---

You want to visit the Globe Theatre in London, where there is a special Shakespeare exhibition.

Listen to the recorded telephone message and complete the notes with a word or number.

SHAKESPEARE GLOBE EXHIBITION

Exhibition open every day from [am | **1**] to 5pm

Admission charges: Adults: £7.50

           Students and senior citizens: [£ | **2**]

           children aged 5 to 15: £5

           [| **3**] ticket: £23

If there are [| **4**] or more in your group, you must book before you come.

The new season will start in [| **5**]

Audioscript

Thank you for calling the Shakespeare Globe exhibition. I'm afraid no-one is available to take your call just now. The exhibition, which includes a guided tour into the theatre, is open from 10am to 5pm daily.

Admission charges are £7.50 for adults, £6 for seniors and students and £5 for children aged 5–15. A family ticket is available for £23. This covers up to 2 adults and 3 children. Groups of 15 or more must book in advance and are eligible for special admission rates. However, we do not take bookings for individuals.

The Globe Theatre season has finished for this year. The new season will be announced in February and will begin in May.

Adapted from *CELS Handbook* (University of Cambridge Local Examinations Syndicate)

---

of specific details such as dates, numbers, prices, and other everyday words which they should know at this level. As with other types of listening text, a lot of what the candidates hear is redundant information, and they have plenty of time to write down answers as they listen. They should use their preparation time before the first listening to read through the task and predict the kind of answer that is required in each gap; for example, in the above text the first answer is a time of the morning, the second is an amount of money in pounds, and so on. The more students practise these kinds of exercise, the easier they will find it to predict the sorts of answers that this task demands. Correct spelling is not essential, except where a word has actually been spelt out on the recording, but students are expected to use symbols appropriately (five pounds, for example, should be written '£5' with the pound sign in front of the number, not after it) and capital letters (for example, when writing names of people, months, countries, and the like).

Regular short dictations of numbers (including telephone numbers), dates, prices, and suchlike are a very useful way of preparing students for this kind of task. A good approach is to start by dictating numbers or words in isolation, and build up to embedding them in sentences, while requiring students simply to write down the particular piece of information that is the focus of the exercise.

Low-level speaking

Speaking tests at low levels tend to be very short (five to ten minutes) but despite this, they tend to be the part of the exam that students fear most. Giving them plenty of practice, and explaining exactly what will happen on the day, will help to allay these anxieties. It is useful to discuss what the candidate should say, and how they should behave, on entering and leaving the exam room. Practising beforehand will help them to feel more confident of knowing what the format of the exam will be, how the examiner will speak to them, and how they should respond to questions and instructions. If possible, it is better to ask a colleague to take the role of 'examiner' in a practice test; they can give more objective feedback on how the student has performed, and the situation is more realistic for the student than if their own teacher is playing the 'examiner' role.

Typically, speaking exams consist of a series of short tasks which assess the candidate's ability to do some or all of the following:

- understand and use everyday expressions for greeting and leave-taking
- exchange basic personal information
- express likes and dislikes, exchange opinions, agree and disagree
- give information, such as describing a picture or talking about a hobby
- take part in a simple role-play, for example, in a shop or at the bus station
- follow instructions
- ask for repetition or clarification

Candidates should expect to be tested on their ability to spell and to say numbers correctly. For example, they may be asked to spell the name of the street where they live, or to say their telephone number.

The language used by the examiner is carefully controlled. Examiners often use a script to ensure that they use appropriate language and treat all candidates equally.

Short exchanges: questions and answers

Straightforward personal questions tend to be used early on in the exam to put candidates at their ease. Examples might be:

- Where are you from?
- Where do you live now? What's your address?
- What do you do? Are you a student, or do you have a job?
- Do you have any brothers and sisters? Tell me about your family.
- How do you travel to school every day? How long is the journey?
- How long have you been learning English?
- Why do you want to learn English?

 Personal questions – students can be asked to think of questions they would ask someone they were meeting for the first time, and their suggestions written on the board (they will almost certainly come up with the sorts of questions that the examiner will ask). The teacher, with the class, should discuss some ways of answering the questions in more than just one or two words. Each student then chooses one question and writes it on a card. As far as possible, all the students should have different questions. The students go round the class, asking their question to as many different people as possible, and answering other people's questions. Their answers should be as full and interesting as possible. At the end, students can say who gave the most interesting answer to their question, and what it was. As a variation or follow-up to this activity, a fluent English speaker can be asked the same questions and their answers recorded for the students to listen to.

Simple conversational exchanges may be introduced by giving candidates an instruction, either to elicit a question or to request a response. The examples shown below are at CEF level A1 (ALTE Breakthrough level). In the City and Guilds Pitman exam, the interlocutor selects just two Type A (eliciting questions) and two Type B (requesting responses) items from a larger range of options.

Type A
- I'm your friend. Ask me the time.
- It's my birthday.   What do you say?
- You want to find a post office. Ask me.

From a City and Guilds Pitman Preliminary Level exemplar question

Type B
- We are in a café. I'm a waiter. You're a customer.
  Good morning. What would you like to drink?
- We're friends.
  Hello. How are you?
- I'm a tourist in your town.
  Excuse me, where's the station, please?

Students taking a speaking exam which includes this activity need to be familiar with the form of instruction given, since this is a rather unnatural way of interacting, which does not happen when people exchange conversation in real life. However, it is very formulaic and can be easily practised in class.

Prompts are used in some speaking exams to assess candidates' ability to ask questions. In the following example, the candidates, who are being examined in pairs, must ask each other questions.

A, here is some information about **a shop which sells CDs.** (Turn to page 123.)

B, you don't know anything about **the shop** so ask **A** some questions about it.

CD MARKET

♦ address?

♦ large / small?

♦ closed / Saturdays?

♦ kind of music?

♦ telephone number?

Adapted from
KET Practice Tests Plus
by Peter Lucantoni (Longman)

Do you understand?

Now **B**, ask **A** your questions about **the CD shop** and **A**, you answer them.

Candidate A – your answers

Asking and answering questions – the teacher finds or creates two short texts, such as the CD Market advertisement above (any kind of information leaflet or notice will do), and makes copies. With the students divided into two groups, A and B, each student in Group A receives one text and each student in Group B receives the other. The students are told to write five questions which can be answered from the information given in their text. They should write the questions on a separate piece of paper, not on the text itself. When they are ready, all students find a partner from the other group. Each student gives their text to their partner and asks them the questions they have prepared. This can be repeated a few times, or the activity can be further developed.

 Prompted questions and answers – this time, the students are in groups of three, and a different text has been given to each person in the group. Each student reads their text and thinks of five questions, but instead of writing the whole question, they just write a prompt. Students then pass their text, and their set of prompts, to the person sitting on their left. This person passes the text on again to the third person in the group, but keeps the prompts. They use the prompts to ask questions, and the person with the text tries to answer them.

Longer speaking turns

In the Trinity Spoken English exams, at all but the lowest (Initial) level, candidates have to **give a short talk** (for two minutes) on a prepared topic. They have a free choice of topic, to allow them to talk about something they are interested in and give them an opportunity to display the language they know. When they have finished their talk, the examiner develops the topic into a conversation. Candidates are strongly advised to use a picture, object, or other visual aid to illustrate their topic. They must not speak from prepared notes, nor appear to have learned their talk by heart.

In other exams, candidates often have to **describe a picture** which the examiner gives them. This kind of task requires the student to sustain a longer speaking turn and use a range of language patterns and vocabulary. They should describe everything they can see, in as much detail as possible. Classroom activities which encourage learners to observe, describe, and paraphrase when they do not know the exact word for something, are good preparation for this activity.

 Students can be asked to find a picture in a magazine or newspaper, bring it to class, display it, and talk about it for one minute. This could become a regular activity, so that each week a certain number of students are responsible for bringing a picture. The pictures can also be used to develop vocabulary, build interview scenarios, or do writing activities.

Hesitating and asking for clarification

Students preparing for lower-level speaking tests need to understand that nobody expects their spoken English to be flawless and fluent. One way to demonstrate that even good speakers of English hesitate and have difficulty expressing themselves, is for the teacher to record herself in a lesson describing or explaining something, and listen to this recording with the students. This can be a good lead-in to a discussion of the strategies that can be used to keep speaking when the speaker cannot think of a word or to clarify an instruction from the examiner that has not been fully understood. Students need to know that it is acceptable to ask the examiner to repeat or clarify information, and that they will gain credit for appropriately managing these difficult moments.

It helps to prepare candidates for speaking tests by arranging for them to do a practice test, in the conditions that will exist on the exam day and, if possible, with the examiner's role taken by a teacher other than their usual class teacher. Supportive feedback from this relative stranger on the way in which a candidate presents him- or herself and behaves during the test, as well as on the quality of the performance itself, can help to address difficulties and reduce the anxiety of the day itself.

Low-level grammar and vocabulary

At lower levels, exam preparation can easily fit within the framework of general English courses; the language that candidates at these levels are supposed to know is limited, and the knowledge and skills tested reflects what is taught in most elementary and lower-intermediate textbooks.

Students are expected to know those items of vocabulary and functional expression which typically occur in the everyday language of speakers of English. These include words and phrases relating to the home, workplace, family, places, hobbies, travel, holidays, likes and dislikes, shopping, food and drink, parts of the body, animals, sport, education, and so on.

Grammar and vocabulary are tested indirectly through reading, writing, listening, and speaking activities which require varying levels of accuracy and appropriacy, as specified in the criteria for each task. The grammatical areas which students should be familiar with at level 2 include the main regular and irregular verb forms and tenses, modal verbs, conditionals, reported speech, question formation, comparative and superlative forms of adjectives and adverbs, countable and uncountable nouns, pronouns, determiners ('a/an' and 'the'), prepositions and prepositional phrases, common phrasal verbs, and connectives.

Conclusions

In this chapter we have:
- considered the aims and special features of lower-level exams.
- discussed the different task types used in lower-level exams.
- looked at the kinds of reading, writing, listening, and speaking skills which are assessed in lower-level exams.
- highlighted the relationship between reading and writing.
- provided sample tasks and classroom activities to practise a range of skills, strategies, and task types.
- addressed the role of grammar and vocabulary in lower-level exams.

Task File

Introduction

- The exercises in this section all relate to topics discussed in the chapter to which the exercises refer. Some expect definite answers, while others only ask for the reader's ideas and opinions.
- Tutors can decide when it is appropriate to use the tasks in this section. Readers on their own can work on the tasks at any stage in their reading of the book.
- The material in the Task File can be photocopied for use in limited circumstances. Please see the note on the inside front cover for photocopying restrictions.

How to be a successful exams teacher

A What is special about teaching an exam class? Pages 1–3

Make a list of differences between exam classes and non-exam classes. How different are they, in your opinion?

EXAM CLASSES	NON-EXAM CLASSES

Say whether you agree or disagree with the following statements. If possible, discuss them with a colleague. If you disagree with any of the statements, rewrite them to reflect your own opinion.

1 Teaching an exam class is easier than teaching a non-exam class because the learners are more motivated.
2 Learners in exam classes make more demands on the teacher than learners in non-exam classes.
3 You will be a better exam class teacher if you liked taking exams yourself when you were at school.
4 In an exam class, all the work should be exam-focused.
5 If a student fails an exam, it is the teacher's fault.

B Building students' exam skills   Pages 8–11

How would you help these students develop better study habits?

1 Student A makes very similar mistakes in all his written work. When you return his homework, he checks the mark, then puts it away in his file and doesn't look at it again.
2 Student B comes to you at the end of every class to ask you to explain bits of vocabulary from her out-of-class reading.
3 Student C completes homework exercises on grammar and vocabulary, but never hands in an essay.
4 Student D started the course well, but seems to have lost interest and is missing some lessons.
5 Student E failed the speaking part of his exam last year, and is worried that he will do so again this year.
6 Student F gets her older brother to help her with her homework, and her results are much better than when she works on her own in class.

Balancing teaching and testing   Pages 11–13

Which of the following activities are 'teaching' and which are 'testing'?
1 Filling in gaps in a written text.
2 Organizing vocabulary into meaning groups.
3 Predicting the content of a reading text.
4 Answering true/false questions about some listening material.
5 Discussing the grammar of a set of example sentences with similar meaning.
6 Writing a timed essay.
7 Reading a piece of dialogue aloud.
8 A multiple choice exercise on prepositions.
9 Brainstorming ideas for an essay.

TASK FILE
Chapter 2

How to plan an exam course and choose materials

A Choosing a coursebook   Pages 20–23

List information about an exam class you may have to teach, as illustrated in the example class profile in Chapter 2 (see page 16). What sort of coursebook do you need for this class? Tick the following if they seem necessary, and put a cross if not important.

'motivators', such as songs and games		explanations in students' first language	
grammar reference sections		a balance of exam and non-exam material	
vocabulary listed by topic		lots of exam-style practice tests	
model answers to writing questions		exam tips for students	
tapescripts in the students' book		accompanying online or CD-ROM material	
units which can be done in a single lesson		a self-study workbook	

B Comparing published course materials   Pages 20–23

Using the information provided in publishers' catalogues (available on their websites), make notes in a grid comparing five different exam course packages.

Title of course and publisher	Exam(s)	Range of materials included	Particular focus (if any)
1			
2			
3			
4			
5			

Based on this information, which of these coursebooks would you be likely to choose for your class? If none are suitable, why not, and what would you do about that?

C Using practice test material   Pages 24–25

Read the following comments by teachers about how they use practice tests. Which of them do you think has the best approach, and why? Are the different approaches suitable for different sorts of students or courses?

I give my students a test, using real exam questions from past papers, right at the start of their course. I do this to give them a feel of what the exam is like, and how near or far they are to knowing enough English to pass it. They quite often find it a bit scary! After that we do some kind of exam practice every week, so that the students get used to the sorts of tasks they will have to do in the exam.

I don't believe in testing my students too much, so we don't do any practice tests until a couple of weeks before the exam. For most of the course we concentrate on general skills improvement, although they do more reading and writing than if they were on a non-exam course, because there is a lot of reading and writing in the exam.

I base all my lessons on material from practice tests. The students do an exercise and then we discuss it together. Afterwards I do short presentations of language points which they have had trouble with. The stuff I teach is all based on the mistakes that they make.

How to teach reading for exams

A Developing exam reading skills   Pages 40–42

Read the following pieces of advice on how to develop the skills needed for exam reading. Put a tick beside each piece of **good** advice and a cross beside each piece of **bad** advice. Rewrite the bad advice so that it becomes good advice.

1 ❑ You can safely ignore the title of the text. It is only there for decoration.
2 ❑ Always start by reading the text slowly and carefully all the way through.
3 ❑ Don't worry about difficult words when you are reading a text for the first time.
4 ❑ If a word seems to be important, always stop and look it up in a dictionary.
5 ❑ In multiple choice questions, start by trying to think of the answers yourself before you look at the four options.
6 ❑ In a text with gaps, make sure that the word you put into each gap is in the right form. Check that it fits grammatically with the words before and after the gap.
7 ❑ It is important to do plenty of timed practice so that you learn how to read fast.
8 ❑ Don't put down an answer unless you are completely sure that it is correct.

B Developing task and strategy awareness   Pages 29–34 & 41–42

Find a practice test for the exam you are interested in. (Past papers are available from the exam board, and most exam coursebooks also include at least one practice test.) Look at the questions which test reading. Put a tick on the list below against each of the task types that appears on the paper.

* Multiple choice
* True/false
* Matching
* Gapped texts
* Proofreading
* Other

Then choose one of the exercise types, do it yourself, and take careful note of what strategies you are using to work out the answers. When you have finished, compare the procedure you used with the ones suggested in the section headed 'Specific procedures and strategies'. To what extent did your procedure match those? How successful were you? How would you rewrite the notes on page 41 for students trying to do this type of exercise?

Simplifying tasks   Pages 35–36

Choose a reading text and task from a past paper or practice test. Simplify the task in at least two of the ways suggested on page 35. Get your students to do the task and monitor success and any difficulties they experience. What further changes would be needed to make it possible for your students to perform the task successfully?

Simplifying texts   Pages 36–37

Find an unabridged feature article (500–800 words) from a newspaper or magazine. Highlight the parts of the text you would need to edit in order to make the text suitable for use with your exam students. Note what kinds of modifications you would need to make. Are all of these mentioned in the list of areas to consider when simplifying texts on page 36?

TASK FILE Chapter 4

How to teach writing for exams

A Applying assessment criteria   Pages 49–50

Assess the two sample answers below. In which mark band (1–5) would you put the two answers? What comments would you make? Use the following criteria, which relate to CEF level B2 (ALTE level 3).

The top mark (5) shows full realization of the task set with all content points included and appropriately expanded; a wide range of vocabulary and structure; minimal errors and well-developed control of language; effective organization of ideas with a variety of linking devices; consistently appropriate register and format. Fully achieves the desired effect on the target reader. The bottom mark (1) is a poor attempt at the task with major omissions and/or irrelevance; narrow range of vocabulary and structure; frequent errors which obscure communication; lack of organization; little or no awareness of register and format. Has a very negative effect on the target reader.

Task: A student magazine is offering a prize for the best article with the title, 'My favourite place'. Write your article in 120–180 words.

Script 1: (from the Longman Learner corpus)

I have always wanted a place, where I could feel free, without being affraid of people's opinion. That's why I have chosen "Hades" The restaurant is situated at 12, Peowizkar street in the centre of Lublin. Apart from this "Hades" is famous for its old cellars. I like this place because there is a pleasant service and you can run into many famous people like artists, musicians, painters even politicians. Besides the manager of 'Hades' arranges a few unique performances, small festivals etc. As you see it is the best place, where you can enjoy yourself and have a good time with friends. If you are sensitive, romantic person and you are interested in new trends of music, arts - you can find it there. I wish that a lot of restaurants and pubs in Poland weren't closed too early. I hope it will change in the future.

Script 2: (from the Longman Learner corpus)

I don't know where my favourite place is situated. I suppose it is somewhere in south-west Europe. The house of my dreams should be very close to a see. Moreover it should be surrounded by a forest and would be not far from a big town. I would like to live in a two-storeyed house with a garret and terrace. There would be a sauna, body building room, swimming pool, big library and room for dancing in my house. In this house would be rooms the same ordinary houses of course, e.g. bath, bedroom, kitchen. In front of my house would be a garden with plenty of flowers, trees and fruit-trees. At the back of this house would be stairways to a private beach, where yacht would be wait for me. I would like to have an Alsatian and a cat. More on ting - red cabriolet (obviously Ferrari) in a garage, possibly Pontiac (a big comfortable american car) Is it too much or too little? As far as I'm concerned, it is enough for me.

B Understanding difficulties with writing   Pages 51–61

Look at the writing section of a past paper of the exam you are working with. Write answers to the questions, adhering strictly to the time and word limit. If possible, get a colleague to grade your work or compare your answers to sample marked answers in the exam handbook. What grade would your answer receive? Which (if any) of the following difficulties did you experience?

I couldn't write within the word limit – I couldn't integrate all the input – I couldn't complete the task(s) within the time limit – I found the task(s) uninspiring – I couldn't think of any ideas – I didn't have time to revise my work – I was unfamiliar with the layout conventions of the genre – I misunderstood the task rubric – other (what?)

How different are your problems from those of your students? If you are at the same proficiency level as your students in a language other than English, repeat this task in that language. (Better still, get hold of a past paper or practice exam with a writing test for that language and actually do the writing tasks.) How do the problems you experience in the two languages differ?

How to teach grammar and vocabulary for exams

A Gap-fill exercises   Page 65

Work through the following IELTS exercise. Observe very carefully how you work out which word fits into each of the gaps in the text. If possible, put a tape recorder close by and talk aloud about what you are doing. When you have finished, consider the following questions:

- How long did the exercise take? How long do you think it would take a student?
- What strategies did you use to complete the exercise? How successful were they?
- Was there any part of it that you found particularly easy or difficult?
- Do you think a dictionary would have helped you at all? If so, how?

Then write down some ideas for helping students with this kind of question.

Complete the summary by choosing answers from the list of words in the box.

Dr Adrianne Hardman explains that it is (1) .... to follow a special programme at a gym in order to improve your health. Research has shown that doing everyday household tasks can (2) .... the risk of serious disease. It has also been found that, (3) .... to popular opinion, several short periods of exercise are as beneficial as longer ones. This is especially good news for those who (4) .... take exercise, because they are likely to experience the greatest benefits. Dr Hardman takes issue with traditional advice, which emphasises the need for (5) .... activity, believing that this (6) .... many people. Her overall message is that it isn't essential to be (7) .... in order to be healthy, we simply need to be more (8) ....

LIST OF WORDS

prevents	regular	discourages	rarely	according	important
helps	fit	lessen	unnecessary	careful	contrary
frequently	vigorous	increase	gentle	active	suits

From *Focus on IELTS* by O'Connell (task instruction and numbering has been modified)

B Recognizing different sorts of learner errors   Pages 69–71

Apply the following correction code to indicate different sorts of errors in the piece of writing shown. If possible, get a colleague to do the task too, and compare marks.

WF word form   ID idiom or fixed expression   DIS discourse (use of connectors)
WG word grammar   ST style or register   GR grammar   SP spelling

The strangest thing about my grandfather is his incredible curiousness. As older he gets, so more questions he likes to ask. He desires to know everything about you, even in case he has never met you before. Sometimes I am afraid to accompany with him on a journey by bus or train, because I die with embarassment every time when he insists to talk with another passengers. Although he gets old now, my grandfather's memory is like an elephant, and he never forgets that what he learns. He always says that life is short and before he dies he must learn something new in every minute. He is a very amazing person!

TASK FILE
Chapter
6

How to teach listening for exams

A Exploring differences between exam listening and listening to spontaneous informal speech   Page 79

Listen to some of the tasks on the cassette or CD accompanying an exam course you are using. What differences do you notice between the recording and spontaneous informal speech? Compare the differences you noted to the list on page 79.

B Understanding the importance of prediction   Pages 85–86

Continue each of the following scripts in your own words to produce a self-contained text. How easy or difficult was it for you to do this? If you speak a foreign or second language at the same proficiency level as your students, ask a native speaker to prepare a similar task in that language. What differences did you find in your ability to complete the scripts?

1 The train on Platform 11 is the …
2 It is with great pleasure that I welcome you here today.
3 You have phoned Clare and Martin.
4 Speaker A: Excuse me. Is there a club called Vampy's somewhere around here?
   Speaker B: …
5 Speaker A: Hi. I'm just coming out of the station. Is there anything you want from the shop?
   Speaker B: …
6 A: If you'd just take a seat, Sasha will be with you in a moment. Can I …

C Developing exam strategies   Pages 85–93

Which of the following do students need to do in the exam? Why? Why not?

1 Make sure they understand every word.
2 Read the instructions.
3 Try and predict what they are going to hear.
4 Wait till the recording has finished before they try to answer the questions.
5 Write their answers on the answer sheet the first time they listen.
6 Skip any questions they are not sure about.
7 Check that their answers don't contain any spelling or grammar mistakes.

D Developing note-taking skills   Pages 88–90

Make a list of the difficulties learners experience with notetaking or sentence-completion exam tasks. What strategies would you suggest for overcoming these difficulties?

How to teach speaking for exams

Working with interlocutor scripts   Page 100

You will need a colleague to help you with this task. Ask your colleague to play the role of the interlocutor, and tell them to read from the following script. Answer each question, imagining you were an exam candidate (this script is based on material from the CAE and CPE interlocutor scripts printed in the Cambridge ESOL exam handbooks). How different are the questions and your responses to those of people meeting for the first time in a social or professional setting such as a party or a conference?

Good morning/afternoon. My name is ... . And your name is ... ?
First of all, I'd like to know a little about you.
Where do you live?
What do you enjoy about living there?
Could you tell me something about why you decided to teach English?
What do you enjoy most about your work?
Apart from languages, what other skills do you think it will be important to learn in the future?
How ambitious are you?
What interesting things have you done recently?
Looking back on your life, what do you consider to be the most memorable event?
Thank you.

Developing coping strategies for the exam room   Pages 108–116

What linguistic patterns would you teach students taking intermediate level exams, to deal with the following situations?

1 They don't understand what they have been asked to do.
2 They didn't hear what somebody said.
3 They don't know the correct word for something.
4 They can't think of anything to say about a picture.
5 They are in the middle of speaking when their mind goes blank.
6 They disagree with an opinion expressed by another candidate or by the interlocutor.
7 They feel that another candidate is talking too much and not letting them say anything.
8 They realize that they have made a mistake and want to correct it.

**TASK FILE
Chapter
8**

How to teach for low-level exams

A What's different about lower-level exams? Page 121

List as many differences as you can think of between lower-level exams (CEF levels A2 and B1 / ALTE levels 1 and 2) and higher-level exams (CEF levels B2 to C2 / ALTE levels 3 to 5).

B Giving feedback on written work Pages 131–132

Decide which errors you would focus on giving feedback to a student at CEF level B1 (ALTE level 2) who produced the piece of writing below. The task was to write 100 words to finish a letter beginning, *Dear Pablo, I had a great day out last week* and including information about where they went, who they went with, and what they did.

Dear Pablo
I had a great day out last week. I and my friend we have decided to visit the London Zoo. We arrived to there at 11 am and first we must pay a ticket. The queue was too long but finally we could buy it and also we took one map. We were lucky to see the penguins when they ate some fish by the hand from the man. The elephants made us laughing with their funny games which they were playing when they were taking bath. But my favorite was the tiger, when he made a big noise and he show so many tooths. I was a little bit fear! This has been my best day of my holiday because you know that I love the animals – I enjoy very much this day. What about you? Do you have so good time like me? Please send me your letter.
Love Freddy

C Preparing lower-level students for speaking tests Pages 138–141

What advice would you give to these low-level students about their speaking test?

1 If we practise speaking in small groups I will pick up my classmates' mistakes.
2 I get very nervous waiting to go into the exam room.
3 I'm afraid that the examiner will speak too fast and I won't understand.
4 Sometimes my mind goes blank and I can't think of the word I need.
5 I know I can do well in the written part of the exam, but my speaking is really weak.

Exams overview

.TE levels and the Common European Framework

ALTE (http://www.alte.org) stands for The Association of Language Testers in Europe. The association is made up of the leading exam providers representing 24 different languages, who are working together to develop a framework of comparison between exams in these different languages. The ALTE framework defines six levels of language ability (Breakthrough, 1, 2, 3, 4, and 5 – see table below). Each ALTE level is further defined through a comprehensive set of 'can-do' statements (examples shown in table), which describe what a typical language user at each level can do in different types of context. The level of difficulty of an examination can be defined by its assignment to one of the six ALTE levels, and these levels are aligned with the Common European Framework of reference for languages: learning, teaching, assessment (CEF). The **CEF** is the outcome of work conducted over many years by the Council of Europe to establish equivalences in the teaching and learning of different languages, which can then inform the development of curricula and materials and define levels of achievement. Most exam boards are now using either the CEF or ALTE levels to describe their exams. When referring to levels in this book we give the CEF level followed by the ALTE level in brackets.

CEF level	ALTE level	Description
C2	5	The capacity to deal with material which is academic or cognitively demanding, and to use language to good effect at a level of performance which may in certain respects be more advanced than that of an average native speaker. *Example: CAN scan texts for relevant information, and grasp main topic of text, reading almost as quickly as a native speaker.*
C1	4	The ability to be communicative with the emphasis on how well it is done, in terms of appropriacy, sensitivity, and the capacity to deal with unfamiliar topics. *Example: CAN deal with hostile questioning confidently. CAN get and hold on to his/her turn to speak.*
B2	3	The capacity to achieve most goals and express oneself on a range of topics. *Example: CAN show visitors around and give a detailed description of a place.*
B1	2	The ability to express oneself in a limited way in familiar situations and to deal in a general way with non-routine information. *Example: CAN ask to open an account at a bank, provided that the procedure is straightforward.*
A2	1	An ability to deal with simple, straightforward information and to begin to express oneself in familiar contexts. *Example: CAN take part in a routine conversation on simple predictable topics.*
A1	Breakthrough	A basic ability to communicate and exchange information in a simple way. *Example: CAN ask simple questions about a menu and understand simple answers.*

From *VALTE framework* (ALTE Secretariat)

The range of exams

Here is a list of the main English language exams, organized in terms of their key focus, such as general English, business English etc. To see how the exams match with the ALTE and CEF levels, see the Exams and Levels table on the inside back cover.

General English Exams

• **University of Cambridge ESOL Main Suite**
(http://www.cambridgeesol.org) – these are general English exams at all levels:

Cambridge Key English Test (KET)
Cambridge Preliminary English Test (PET)
Cambridge First Certificate in English (FCE)
Cambridge Certificate in Advanced English (CAE)
Cambridge Certificate of Proficiency in English (CPE)

- **Cambridge ESOL Certificates in English Language Skills** (CELS) (http://www.cambridgeesol.org) – these are a modular suite of exams offering separate assessment of each skill (reading, writing etc) at three levels:
CELS Preliminary
CELS Vantage
CELS Higher

- **London Tests of English** (http://www.edexcel-international.org) – these exams are often particularly suitable for learners on short courses:
Foundation
Elementary
Intermediate
Upper Intermediate
Advanced
Proficient

- **The University of Michigan: English Language Institute exams** (http://www.lsa.umich.edu/eli) – these exams in American English are more or less equivalent in level and type to the Cambridge First Certificate and Proficiency exams:
Examination for the Certificate of Competency in English (ECCE)
Examination for the Certificate of Proficiency in English (ECPE)

- **City and Guilds Pitman International English qualifications** (http://www.pitmanqualifications.com) – these exams offer particular flexibility to schools who want to arrange exams outside the main examining periods:
International ESOL (English for Speakers of Other Languages)
International SESOL (Spoken English for Speakers of Other Languages)

- **Trinity ESOL exams** (http://www.trinitycollege.co.uk) – exams in spoken English are available at twelve levels, and integrated skills exams at three levels.
Trinity Spoken English Exams
Trinity Integrated Skills in English (ISE)

Academic English Exams

- **International English Language Testing System (IELTS)** (http://www.ielts.org) – these exams are jointly administered by Cambridge ESOL, the British Council, and IDP Education Australia (http://www.idp.org). All candidates take the same listening and speaking modules, but there is a choice in reading and writing between Academic and General Training modules. Candidates who intend to study in the medium of English at a further education college or university take the Academic modules. Candidates who are taking IELTS to show that their level of English is good enough for secondary education or work training in an English-speaking environment take the General Training modules.

- **Test of English as a Foreign Language (TOEFL)**
  (http://www.ets.org/toefl) – this exam measures the ability of candidates to understand American English well enough to undertake college or university study, primarily in the United States.

  TOEFL scores are quoted as three-figure numbers, ranging between 310 and 677 for the paper-based test, and 40 to 300 on the computer-based test. A score of 550 on the paper-based test equates to 213 on the computer-based test. 550/213 is the score generally regarded as a necessary minimum for entry to university programmes.

English for Business and Work Purposes

- **Cambridge Business English Certificates (BEC)**
  (http://www.cambridgeesol.org) – these exams have a business focus but are similar in format to the Cambridge main suite exams. There are three levels:
  BEC Preliminary
  BEC Vantage
  BEC Higher

- **Test of English for International Communication (TOEIC)**
  (http://www.ets.org/toeic) – this is an American English paper-based exam particularly recognized by businesses in the Pacific Rim countries for the recruitment of staff. TOEIC shares with TOEFL and IELTS the characteristic that candidates do not 'pass' or 'fail', but are given a score which may be compared with the standard expected by a specific employer.

- **City and Guilds Pitman Business exams**
  (http:/www.pitmanqualifications.com) – these exams are designed to test the language competence of people working in business contexts or preparing to do so:
  Pitman English for Business Communication
  Pitman Spoken English for Business
  Pitman English for Office Skills

English for Young Learners

- **Cambridge Young Learners English tests**
  (http://www.cambridgeesol.org) – designed for children aged 7 to 12, these exams provide a bridge to the Cambridge main suite exams:
  Starters
  Movers
  Flyers

- **London Tests of English for Children**
  (http://www.edexcel-international.org) – designed for children aged 8 to 13, these exams cover topics of interest to this age group.

- **City and Guilds Pitman Young Learners exams**
  (http://www.pitmanqualifications.com)– designed for children aged 8 to 13, these exams cover topics of interest to this age group:
  Pitman Young Learners English for Speakers of Other Languages (YESOL)
  Pitman Young Learners Spoken English for Speakers of Other Languages (Spoken YESOL)

Index